Franz Joseph Haydn's KEYBOARD SONATAS

an untapped gold mine

*A cassette to accompany this volume
is available from the publisher.*

Franz Joseph Haydn's
KEYBOARD SONATAS

an untapped gold mine

JAMES L. TAGGART

Studies in the History and Interpretation of Music

—Volume Four—

THE EDWIN MELLEN PRESS
LEWISTON/QUEENSTON
LAMPETER

Library of Congress Cataloging-in-Publication Data
Taggart, James L.
　Franz Joseph Haydn's Keyboard Sonatas

　(Studies in the history and interpretation of music ; v. 4)
　　Bibliography: p.
　　Discography: p.
　　Includes index.
　　1. Haydn, Joseph, 1732-1809. Sonatas, piano. I. Title. II. Series.
ML410.H4T25 1988　　786.1'092'4　　88-9282
ISBN 0-88946-430-8

> This is volume 4 in the continuing series
> Studies in the History and Interpretation of Music
> Volume 4 ISBN 0-88946-430-8
> SHIM Series ISBN 0-88946-426-X

Copyright © 1988 James L. Taggart

All rights reserved. For information contact:

The Edwin Mellen Press　　　　　　　The Edwin Mellen Press
P.O. Box 450　　　　　　　　　　　　　P.O. Box 67
Lewiston, New York　　　　　　　　　 Queenston, Ontario
U.S.A. 14092　　　　　　　　　　　　　CANADA L0S 1L0

The Mellen House
Lampeter, Dyfed, Wales
UNITED KINGDOM SA48 7DY

Printed in the United States of America

Table of Contents

Foreword ix
I. Background
    Historical Significance of the Sonatas 1
    Numbering and Publication History 2
    The Instruments 4
II. The Evolution of Form and Style in the Sonatas: A Survey
    From Divertimento to Dramatic Sonata:
        The Early Works 9
    A Romantic Crisis 16
    Reaction and Conflict 26
    Stylistic Maturity: Craft, Humor and Eloquence 41
    Master of the Form:
        The Fruition of a Lifetime Effort 52
III. Teaching the Sonatas: Rewards and Problems
    Selecting a Teaching Edition 69
    The Young and Inexperienced Student 70
    The Intermediate Student 78
    The Mature Student 91
IV. Summary and Conclusion 101
Endnotes 103
Bibliography
    Books, Periodicals and Dissertations 105
    Editions of the Sonatas 107
Discography of Haydn's Sonatas 109
Index of Musical Examples 111
Appendix
    Collation of Sonata Numbers in the Universal
        Edition with Other Editions 113
Index 117

Permission for use of copyrighted musical examples

All musical examples in this book are copied from the Vienna Urtext Edition. A non-exclusive license for use of the examples has been granted to the author, James L. Taggart, by European American Music Distributors (sole U. S. Agent for Vienna Urtext). The following copyright inscriptions apply to specific musical examples as follows:

EXAMPLES 1, 2, 4-7, 47-54, 56-59 and 60
    Covering sonatas 1 through 15)

> Copyright 1981 by Wiener Urtext Edition, Musikverlag Ges.m.b.H. & Co., K.G., Wien. All rights reserved. Used by permission of European American Music Distributors Corporation, sole U.S. agent for Wiener Urtext.

EXAMPLES 3, 8-12 and 65:
    (Covering Sonatas 30 through 33)

> Copyright 1966 by Universal Edition A.G. Wien. Assigned 1973 to Wiener Urtext Edition, Musikverlag Ges.m.b.H. & Co., K.G., Wien. All rights reserved. Used by Permission of European American Music Distributors Corporation, sole U.S. agents for Wiener Urtext.

EXAMPLES 13-46, 55, 61-63 and 66:
    (Covering Sonatas 34 through 62)

> Copyright 1964 by Universal Edition A.G., Wien. Assigned 1973 to Wiener Urtext Edition, Musikverlag Ges. M.G.H. & Co., K.G., Wien. All rights reserved. Used by permission of European American Music Distributors Corporation, sole U.S. Agent for Wiener Urtext.

James Taggart, born in Benton Harbor, Michigan in 1932, was determined to become a pianist from his early years. He studied with John Simms at the University of Iowa, receiving the Bachelor of Music in 1954.

While serving in England as an officer in the United States Air Force, Dr. Taggart studied in London with John Hunt, Fellow of the Royal Academy of Music and pupil of both Arther Schnaebel and Donald Francis Tovey.

After returning to the U.S. in 1957, Dr. Taggart received the Master of Fine Arts in Piano Performance and the Ph.D. in Piano Literature and Performance at the University of Iowa. His long teaching and performing career has included appointments at the University of Nebraska at Omaha and Central State University in Oklahoma. He is presently Professor of Music and Head of the Piano Division at Marshall University in Huntington, West Virginia. He is known in that region for his many lecture-recitals on the works of Haydn, Mozart, and Beethoven, and as both a solo and chamber music performer.

Dr. Taggart's two four-part series of lecture-recitals on the Sonatas of Haydn and Mozart were broadcast over public television station PBYS in Huntington during 1978 and 1979.

Foreword

From the Virginia coast to bluegrass country, I recently "spread the gospel" of Haydn's Sonatas in a three-month series of lecture-recitals. Performing and discussing the Sonatas for all kinds of audiences, I encountered an immediate grasp and appreciation of the craftsmanship, pianism and everlasting beauty of these marvelous works. Yet, in the overall musical scene in this country, there seems to be no real tradition for the study, performance and appreciation of Haydn's Keyboard Sonatas, except as "poor relations" to those of Mozart and Beethoven. Both in the studio and on the concert stage, only a few of the Sonatas seem to appear, and then infrequently.

In the *Music Teachers' National Association* high school auditions, where specific composers and works are often required, Haydn is rarely singled out. In the 1984-85 auditions, the first movement of a Haydn Sonata *was* required, but the choice was limited to those in Volume IV of the 1937 C. F. Peters Edition. This volume contains only two or three of the much larger number of Haydn's Sonatas of great musical and technical value, highly suitable for contests.

A survey of major American periodicals devoted mostly or exclusively to keyboard music and/or keyboard teaching reveals consistent neglect of Haydn's Sonatas. Other than reviews of recordings, only five articles dealing specifically with the Sonatas have appeared in the last thirty years. Two of these deal only with the interpretation for two early Sonatas. Even the quarter-millenium year of Haydn's birth (1982) inspired only one article in the *American Music Teacher*, and that was devoted to the String Quartets.

A pattern of neglect in live performance of Haydn's Sonatas can be inferred from Donald Confletti's article in the January, 1978 *American Music Teacher*, "What Do Pianists Play In New York City?," in which 628 solo programs during the period 1973-1978 were surveyed to determine how frequently certain composers and compositions were programmed. Haydn appeared in only 10% of the programs, while Mozart and Beethoven appeared in 20% and 50% respectively. Only six of Haydn's Sonatas were programmed at all, and only his last *Sonata in E-Flat Major* was played more than ten times. I do not believe these proportions have changed much since then. The apparent neglect of Haydn in teaching, from the early years to the conservatory, is bound to have had its effect on the concert hall.

In contradiction to their abyssimal record in live performance, Haydn's Sonatas appear to have fared well in electronic recordings. Two Austrian pianists, Rudolph Buchbinder (on Telefunken label) and Ilse van Alpenheim (on Vox), have recorded the complete Sonatas. The former is currently out of print, but is available in good music libraries. In 1976, under the Hungaroton label in Budapest, a group of young Hungarian artists issued the complete solo keyboard works of Haydn, including the Sonatas. Also, Vox has issued 50 of the Sonatas in four three-disc sets, with four different artists. There has been at least one other recording of the complete sonatas and a number of releases of selected Sonatas, some in large numbers, by major artists. Among all of these recordings, a growing number of compact disc reprints are being made.

In biographical books surveying Haydn's works stylistically, the sonatas are often discussed only perfunctorily, but they have attracted considerable attention among scholars and musicologists. William S. Newman's book, *The Sonata in the Classical Era*, for example, treats the Sonatas as important works deserving of study and performance. At least five important doctoral dissertations dealing comprehensively with historical, structural or interpretative aspects of the Sonatas have been completed at major American universities in the last forty years. At an *International Haydn Conference* held in Washington, D. C. in 1975, a number of important lectures, papers and workshops were devoted specifically to the Sonatas. (The *Proceedings* of the Conference were published in 1981). And finally, A. Peter Brown's recent book, *Joseph Haydn's Keyboard Works: Sources and Style* (Indiana University Press, 1986) includes detailed historical and theoretical studies of the sonatas.

However, in spite of recording, research, and a limited number of written publications, the overall pattern is one of disproportionate neglect of Haydn's Sonatas. This phenomenon cannot be a result of musical quality. The Sonatas exhibit bold and original strokes of formal design, rich and progressive harmonic and tonal plans, melodic charm and elegance, rhythmic vitality, demanding and idiomatic pianism, and an emotional spectrum that is both broad and deep. Perhaps today's artists feel that the "bigger" pieces of Beethoven, like the "Appassionata" or the "Hammerklavier", more immediately satisfy the "sonata appetites" of modern audiences. Or perhaps the artists themselves have never really appreciated the subtlety, wit and charm that make Haydn so attractive and rewarding to his listeners.

Some historical questions also may help to explain the neglect. Haydn's Sonatas were popular with students and amateur connoisseurs, and at private soirees and salons in his own time. Two-thirds of them were published before his death, an evidently extraordinary statistic for the eighteenth century. They were praised in almost every contemporary review. But because public performance of solo keyboard music was not a general practice until the first decades of the nineteenth century, Haydn's Sonatas remained in relative obscurity for many years after his death. (The same applies to Mozart.) Also, a complete critical edition of the Sonatas did not appear until more than a century after Haydn's death.

Whatever the reasons for Haydn's absence in too many auditions and student recitals and in too many concerts in New York, it is time, I think, for us to revaluate the sonatas historically, aesthetically and pedagogically, if not, indeed, to truly evaluate them for the first time.

* * * * * * *

The writer wishes to acknowledge the following for their contributions and encouragement:

- - - WPBY Television in Huntington, West Virginia, for programming my first four-part lecture-recital series on Haydn's Sonatas, thereby providing the impetus for further investigation of audience reaction to and appreciation of the Sonatas.

- - - Alan Aulabaugh, on the music faculty of Eastern Illinois University in Charleston, Illinois, whose Ph.D. Dissertation on performance problems in Haydn's Sonatas (University of Iowa, 1958) first sparked my abiding interest in the music.

- - - Marshall University, in Huntington, West Virginia, which provided me with a sabbatical leave in 1986 to conduct a tour of Haydn lecture-recital performances that serve as part of the background for this book.

- - - European American Music Corporation in Valley Forge, PA, for permission to use reproductions of Christa Landon's Universal Edition of the Sonatas for musical examples.

- - - Valerie Taggart, for her tolerance in having to live simultaneously, for an unreasonable length of time, with a twentieth-century and an eighteenth-century musician -- one of whom blamed the other for her neglect.

Chapter I

Background

Historical Significance of the Sonatas

For nearly thirty years, Haydn's demanding duties at the court of the Hungarian Prince Nicholaus at Esterhaza included composition on demand, continual conducting, and administrative organization of the extremely active musical life of the court. There resulted hundreds of works -- symphonies, chamber music, operas, and religious music -- in literally a lifetime of constant creativity.

The Symphonies and String Quartets in particular attracted wide public attention in Haydn's time, and have enjoyed to this day unwavering popularity. Yet he still took time to write keyboard sonatas for smaller circles of admirers and students, and for his own creative purposes. As the forms of the symphony and quartet grew and matured in Haydn's hands, so was the keyboard sonata conceived and developed. The form and style of his Sonatas serve as the foundation for much of the keyboard literature from his own time to the present day. Their significance is greatly underestimated by most Haydn biographers and critics.

Partly because of the social and historical conditions in which they were created, Haydn's Sonatas offer a greater amount of repertoire to a wider range of musicians than perhaps any other group of multi-movement, solo keyboard works by a single composer. Composed during a period of more than forty years, the 54 complete Sonatas that have survived serve casual amateurs who possess limited keyboard skills and an avocational zeal for making good music, serious piano students from the early grades to the conservatory, and concert pianists who wish to give their programs an extra measure of charm, wit and vitality.

Aside from their pedagogical and performance values, the Sonatas are a microcosm of Haydn's working methods in the sonata idiom, from their beginings to their zenith. In structure alone, they constitute a comprehensive course in music theory. Also, the evolution of sonata style during the entire

Classical period is mirrored in Haydn's work, which stands out as the superior accomplishment among many.

Haydn's youthful efforts at the keyboard sonata were at first brief, facile suites for students. As experimental exercises in an excitingly new style, the early Sonatas also represent a serious groping for improved formal design and a dramatic sonata idiom. It is known that Haydn did not intend these preliminary exercises to be published,[1] and many other of this genre probably have not survived. We are fortunate, indeed, that the posthumous publication of many of the early Sonatas took place, more or less completing the picture of an amazing lifetime growth in Haydn's Sonata methods. This wonderful opportunity for such a microscopic view of creative development in a single formal type is paralleled in Mozart's Concerti, but nowhere else in the keyboard literature. Beethoven's early Sonatas represent an already mature handling of an established form (although the six "Bonn" Sonatas show some groping, preliminary methods). Mozart hardly labored at all over sonata form, devoting more of his attention to the concerto and almost casually arriving at a masterful command of the accepted, standard sonata - typical of his prodigious genius.

So Haydn emerges, historically, as the one who took the sonata "seeds" sown by a few older contemporaries, watered them, nurtured the growing plants, pruned them, hybridized them, and passed on living organisms to be reproduced and nurtured further by future generations of composers, for nearly 200 years. The original plants are alive and well, and there is no reason to think they will ever die.

Numbering and Publication History

Including lost works identified by thematic incipits in his own catalogues, and one other incomplete autograph, Haydn is known to have composed or started to compose 62 keyboard sonatas. (Further discoveries may well determine the number to be larger). These works span almost his entire creative life, from probably the mid-1750's to the 1790's. Exact dating of the early works is impossible because of lost manuscripts, necessitating reliance upon secondary sources (first editions, autograph copies and catalogues).

The most accurate and complete text of the Sonatas is contained in Christa Landon's three-volume edition, published by Universal Edition in Vienna in 1963, with subsequent editions in 1966 and 1973 (when publication was assigned to Vienna Urtext Edition). This has been easily available in this country for many years and is now handled by European American Music Distributors in Valley Forge, PA. It includes 54 complete sonatas (five of which were previously unpublished), the aforementioned incomplete Sonata, and seven thematic incipits of lost sonatas, for a total of 62 works numbered chronologically. (All musical examples in this book are taken from the Universal Edition).

Landon's educated guesswork about the numbering of early works has really not been challenged, and her extensive prefatory notes covering source materials and interpretation, together with a clear printed text and Oswald Jonas' excellent fingering, make this edition the most valuable for serious students and teachers of Haydn.

The earliest critical edition of the Sonatas was published in 1918 by Breitkopf and Härtel and edited by Karl Päsler.[2] This contained 52 works, three of which have been judged spurious. The Breitkopf and Härtel edition is no longer available, but it was the basis for the practical edition published in 1937 by C. F. Peters and edited by C. A. Martienssen.[3] The Peters edition contains 43 Sonatas in four volumes, and was supplemented in 1952 with an additional volume of six early Sonatas entitled "Six Easy Divertimenti." (The three spurious sonatas in the Päasler edition were excluded). Martienssen's editorial additions of interpretative markings may lack some authenticity, if not stylistic integrity, and there is no attempt at chronological numbering, but as a "working" edition of its time, the Peters publication was for a quarter of a century the most valuable to Haydn enthusiasts who were thrilled to have 49 Sonatas in print. It is still easily available.

A later edition of the Sonatas in which scholarship equals but does not necessarily surpass the Universal Edition was published by G. Henle in Munich in 1972. Edited by the eminent Haydn scholar, Georg Feder, this edition does not attempt to number the early Sonatas chronologically, but rather groups them according to their scope and function, i.e., student or amateur pieces as opposed to those more highly developed for professional musicians. All the complete Sonatas and fragments contained in the Universal Edition are included in the Henle, except the first movement of Universal's No. 57, the authenticity of which is questioned by Feder.[4]

Another European publication is the excellent student edition of selected Sonatas in two volumes, edited by Lajos Hernadi and published by Editio Musico in Budapest. This is available through Boosey and Hawkes in the United States.

Other editions, appearing between the years 1894 and 1959, are somewhat less valuable in terms of editorial scholarship and the number of Sonatas included in each. These are listed in the *Bibliography* (pages 107-108).

In 1957 Anthony van Hoboken published a thematic catalogue (B. Schotts, Mainz) which amounted to the first definitive accounting of all of Haydn's works. Hoboken duplicated Päsler's numbering and dating of 52 keyboard Sonatas in the 1918 Breitkopf and Härtel edition, unfortunately perpetuating the latter's flaws in chronology and in the authenticity of three of the works. Hoboken's Catalogue, with its "H" numbers, nevertheless has become a standard reference for identification of the Sonatas.

My references to the Sonatas correspond numerically with the Universal Edition. In each case the "H" number is also included in parenthesis when a work is first mentioned.[5]

The Instruments

Harpsichord idioms are predominant in at least the first 28 of Haydn's Sonatas and remain an important influence until the very last Sonata. These idioms include: melodic expression through fastidious and refined articulation, rather than dynamic shading; dynamics sharply delineated by phrases or periods, including echo effects; and ornamentation which enlivens long notes. In this passage from the first movement of *Sonata 11 in B-Flat Major* (H. 2), the choice of the harpsichord is fairly obvious:

Example 1. *Sonata 11 in B-Flat Major*, First Movement, Bars 31-43.

Some of the early works seem better suited to the subtle shading of the clavichord, such as the opening passage of the slow movement of the same Sonata:[6]

Example 2. *Sonata 11 in B-Flat Major, Largo*, Bars 1-4

Haydn's manuscripts, for both the early and later Sonatas, usually include the phrase "per il cembalo" (literally, "for the harpsichord") in their titles, with the later works adding "o forte piano" ("or piano" i.e., with its eighteenth-century designation). Haydn's persistent use of the term cembalo, even for late works that are clearly pianistic, seems to indicate its rather loose application, perhaps to designate a choice of any keyboard instrument. Also, the practicality of playing the Sonatas on the harpsichord when a fortepiano was not available may have prompted the usage, especially since the fortepiano then was a modern invention not yet in widespread use or distribution.

The real fortepiano style, with a wider range of shading and more powerful harmonic textures, seems evident at least by the time of *Sonata 30 in D Major* (H. 19) and without any doubt in *Sonata 33 in C Minor* (H. 20), written in 1771. The first movement of the latter Sonata features a sustained opening theme, followed a few bars later by abrupt dynamic changes on six fairly rapid, successive notes that would be both awkward and uncharacteristic on the harpsichord. The choice of fortepiano here is undeniable:

(a) Opening Movement, Bars 1-2   (b) Bars 13-14

Example 3.   *Sonata 33 in C Minor*, First Movement

Throughout this entire movement, Haydn's dynamic markings are so detailed and so pianistic as to demand the use of the more modern instrument.

Since Haydn's keyboard idioms remained somewhat mixed, interpretation on the modern grand piano should attempt to balance them:

widely-graded dynamics and expressive shading (but never to excess) where the powers of the piano best bring out the structure; sustained melodies employing the maximum "singing" quality of the piano where the musical line and expression call for it; careful articulation, little or no pedal, and terrace dynamics where harpsichord style prevails; and ornamentation faithful to the composer's intentions and to eighteenth-century practices at all times.

Chapter II

The Evolution of Form and Style in the Sonatas: A Survey

From Divertimento to Sonata -- The Early Works

Haydn was writing sonatas, as well as symphonies and quartets, in a time of rapid transition, not only in the development of keyboard instruments, but also in the development of musical form and style. About the first half of his Sonatas were actually entitled "divertimento" or "partita". These terms, interchangeable with many other in the mid-eighteenth century, signified multi-movement instrumental pieces of a light, entertaining nature. Most modern editions of Haydn use the title Sonata for all of the multi-movement solo keyboard works, it is supposed, for the convenience of uniformity.

The rococo divertimento, produced in abundance by Viennese composers, including Wagenseil, Monn and others, retained certain Baroque structural methods: motivic play, with short, fragmented themes; ornamental melodic designs; and much sequential repetition. The divertimento style typifies Haydn's early work, as the opening of his very first *Sonata* (H. 8, titled "Partita") testifies:

Example 4. *Sonata 1 in G Major*, First Movement Exposition

Other features of Haydn's early keyboard writing also are consistent with the divertimento: identical tonality for all movements; abundant dance forms, particularly the minuet; mostly homophonic textures with sparse, chordal voicing; and a great deal of notated ornamentation, especially short trills and turns.

However, even though Haydn retained the terms divertimento and partita as titles for all of the works during the 1750's and '60's, and certain elements of the gallant style throughout his life, he moved steadily toward the truly dramatic and broadly expressive sonata almost from the beginning. In *Sonata 4 in G Major* (H. Gl, entitled "Divertimento"), the first movement is in sonata-allegro form, although narrow in scope and not very dramatic. The development section employs the three principal motives from the exposition with somewhat unassuming sequential repetition, but nonetheless an effective and colorful tonal scheme:

Example 5. *Sonata 4 in G Major*, First Movement Development

Of course, sonata-allegro form was not entirely new at this time. Haydn surely was aware of its early development by the previous generation of composers which included Reutter, Wagenseil, Monn, J. S. Bach's sons and others.

The other two movements of *Sonata 4* are distinctly rococo in character: a small minuet and trio and a light-hearted finale in simple ternary form, both in the same key as the opening movement. The whole work lasts only a few minutes, and its ease of keyboard technique, like most of the early Sonatas, suggests student or amateur use.

The term sonata had an indefinite, rather vague meaning in the mid-eighteenth century. Just about any instrumental piece could be called sonata (particularly in Italy), along with other interchangeable titles such as "piece di clavecin" in France and "lesson" in England. As the true sonata *style* emerged, however, certain structural and expressive characteristics became more consistently present. Structure began to focus more on complete melodic phrases rather than on motivic "play," resulting in greater breadth and coherence, as well as more dramatic contrast. The formal concept of "theme" became the norm, with the grouping, repetition and contrast of complimentary phrases into paragraphs and sections. Development replaced motivic play with dramatic devices such as fragmentation, remote modulation, and the combination of expository motives in contrapuntal textures.

The most important aspect of the new style, however, was the wide range of emotions resulting from new concepts of formal design. The "fires" of sonata expressiveness were fed, at least in part, by the mid-eighteenth century romantic movement known in Germany as the "Sturm und Dräng" (Storm and Stress). Unlike the light and entertaining Viennese divertimento, a great many sonatas exhibited the drama, personal expression and colorful textures typical of Sturm and Dräng ideals. One eighteenth-century theorist and scholar, J. A. P. Shultz, described the emotional purpose of the sonata in a 1775 dictionary article in this way:

"Clearly in no form of instrumental music is there a better opportunity than in the sonata to depict feelings without the aid of words. The symphony and the overture have a more fixed character. The form of a concerto seems designed more to give a skillful player a chance to be heard against the background of many instruments than to implement the depiction of violent emotions. Aside from these forms, and the dances, which also have their special characters, there remains only the form of the sonata, which assumes any or all characters and every kind of expression. By means of the sonata, the composer can hope to produce a monologue through tones of melancholy, grief, sorrow, tenderness, or delight and joy; or maintain sensitive dialogue solely through impassioned tones of similar or different qualities; or simply depict emotions that are violent, impetuous, and sharply contrasted; or light, gentle, fluent and pleasing."

Shultz obviously believed that the entire gamut of human experience was appropriate to the expressive range of the sonata, and the music of the time bears him out.

Haydn was in the forefront of this revolutionary change in the instrumental music of the late eighteenth century. In his keyboard works, as in his *Symphonies and Quartets*, he moved quickly, with originality and boldness, in the direction of the sonata, embracing with vigor and imagination the new emotional language described by Shultz.

The contrast of *Sonata 11* with *Sonata 4* (both quoted above) illustrates the rapidity with which Haydn's early sonata style was emerging. *Sonata 11*, probably written a very short time after No. 4, is surprisingly larger in scope and purpose. The development section of its first movement has a new level of intensity pointing toward the extended dramatic designs of the larger works that were to follow:

Example 6. *Sonata 11 in B-Flat Major*, First Movement Development

Sonata 11 contains an expressive *Largo* in the contrasting minor mode which is a prototype of the romantic slow movements in later works, such as *Sonata 13 in G Major* (H. 6) and the five Sonatas of Haydn's "Sturm und Dräng" period (1766-71). The tonal scheme in this *Largo* is greatly expanded, with an abundance of rich harmonic textures such as the following:

Example 7. *Sonata 11 in B-Flat Major, Largo*, Bars 18-28

The *Menuet*, in this case acting as a finale, is highly stylized for the period, anticipating later works in which the minuet has a special kind of personal expression and classical refinement. (Haydn placed a minuet in more than half the sonatas -- as a middle movement in 14 cases and a finale in 15 more, including one as late as *Sonata 59 in E-Flat Major* [H. 49].)

As his pursuit of the sonata continued, Haydn seems to have persisted in two goals: 1) flexibility and originality of structure, and 2) expansion of emotional substance. Although he had little to draw upon by way of previous sonata history, he perfected and refined many types of movements with complete originality. His direct influence probably extended to Clementi, Mozart, Beethoven and Schubert.

Haydn can be credited also with the creation of new forms, such as the rondo-variation hybrid (as in the finale of *Sonata 30 in D Major* [H. 19]) and the variation form with an alternating major-minor theme (as in the *Scherzando* of *Sonata 49 in C-Sharp Minor* [H. 36] or the *Andante* of *Sonata 58 in C Major* [H. 48]). He composed sonatas in two-, three- and four-movement cycles with inconsistent arrangements, although three-movement plans are predominant. His sonata-allegro, or "first-movement" form, grew to great proportions, achieving extreme unity in the economy and conciseness of themes, and a very wide expressive gamut.

Romantic Crisis

The progress of Haydn's love affair with the keyboard sonata was not all sweetness and light, however. At first he embraced the emotionalism of the Sturm und Dräng to excess, composing five increasingly romantic sonatas from 1766 to 1771, culminating in the *C-Minor Sonata*, No. 33 (H. 20). All but one of these, *Sonata 32 in G Minor* (H. 44), has a long, expressive slow movement, and there are no minuets. Four of the first movements are marked *Moderato* or *Allegro moderato*, tempi which accommodate expressive nuance and lyricism (comparing to Schubert's methods). Only one of the finales (No. 30 in D Major) can be categorized as the "jolly" type with which we tend to stereotype Haydn, and three of them are set in sonata-allegro form, or some bybrid of that form and others.

The expressive range and character of these works make all of Haydn's previous sonatas seem like a different world. There is the fairly obvious influence of C. P. E. Bach, especially in *Sonatas 30* and *33*, the first of which was contemporarily criticized as a parody of the older composer. But romantic excesses aside, Haydn made great strides in form and pianism during these years.

A close look at *Sonata 30 in D Major* provides a vivid example of the evolutionary process that rapidly was unfolding. Composed in 1767, the *D-Major Sonata* achieves an amazing stylistic balance in the contrast of its three movements. These consist of: a lyrical sonata-allegro with an intensely dramatic development section; an *Andante* that exhudes simplicity and charm, but great ingenuity in the exploitation of different pianistic colors and registers; and the one finale in the five "romantic" works that has a light, jocular character, perfectly balancing the other movements. In short, the work is a masterpiece. The following excerpts give a tantalizing glimpse of what the Sonata is all about: (a) from the development section of the first movement, (b) showing the use of the "cello" register of the piano for maximum lyrical effect in the slow movement, and (c) the opening of the jolly finale:

(a) First Movement, Development Section, Bars 52-67

(b) *Andante*, Bars 32-49

(c) *Finale*, Bars 1-6

Example 8. *Sonata 30 in D Major*

Sonata 31 in A-Flat Major (H. 46) has an even more lyrical opening movement. Its singing lines and long phrases of irregular length are shown in Example 9, where the five phrases are successively 3, 2-1/2, 2-1/2, 2 and 2 bars long, resulting in an extremely rhetorical character:

Example 9. *Sonata 31 in A-Flat Major*,
First Movement, Bars 1-12

The ornamental melodic style of the rococo still underlies Haydn's writing here, but the broad thematic layout is in obvious contrast to his earlier methods. This movement is perhaps the most lyrical and melodically elegant of all the Sturm und Drang works.

The *Adagio* adds to the lyricism, with a three-voice contrapuntal texture reminiscent of some of Bach's loveliest sarabandes and arias:

Example 10. *Sonata 31 in A-Flat Major, Adagio*,
Bars 29-40

In this *Adagio*, as well as in the slow movement of the previous *Sonata in D Major, No. 30*, there are fermatae on a I $^6_4$ chord preceding the final phrase. As a matter of tradition in much of the instrumental music of the eighteenth century, short cadenzas were improvised at these points. In such cases, both the C. F. Peters and Universal editions provide suggested cadenzas in footnotes to the score, although performers may create their own. The resulting personal touch thus serves to further enhance the romantic nature of these works.[7]

The finale of the *A-Flat Sonata* returns to a more fragmented, motivic structure, but with a serious and dramatic purpose. All three movements of this work are in sonata-allegro form, maintaining a high level of intensity throughout. It is difficult to find a more appealing Haydn Sonata in terms of melodic beauty, harmonic richness, emotional range and structural balance.

Sonata 33 in C Minor (H. 20) represents the extreme to which Haydn was to carry his preoccupation with the Sturm und Drang in his keyboard works. This work, the earliest one actually bearing the title "Sonata," exhibits the greatest influence of C.P.E. Bach. Tension and pathos abound throughout, with many sudden changes of mood (a la Beethoven!), dramatic, rhetorical pauses, notated changes of tempo (with some implied rubato), and almost improvizational keyboard writing. All of these characteristics are combined in the first 26 bars of the first movement:

Example 11. *Sonata 33 in C Minor*, First Movement, Bars 1-26

Ornaments in the *C-Minor Sonata*, especially in the first two movements, are more abundant than in earlier, rococo works. But here they seem to function more as integral parts of the melodic line. Pianistic idioms are greatly advanced, with sustained note values, and for the first time in the Sonatas, notation of graded dynamics in surprising detail. (There is some speculation that dynamic markings may have been added at the time of the first edition of the Sonata in 1780, nine years after its composition.)

In contrapuntal technique, the slow movement of the *C-Minor Sonata* resembles the *Adagio* in the *A-Flat Major Sonata* (Example 10). In spite of the serene character of the melodies taken individually, the constant syncopation of the voices after the opening statement maintains a kind of rhythmic tension throughout the movement, resulting in an unsettled mood consistent with the entire Sonata. The syncopation also implies a kind of rhythmic freedom, whereby delays of one hand behind the other are not intended to be exactly as notated, but rather to quicken or lengthen as the shape of the phrase dictates.[8] The middle of the movement, where the syncopation becomes the most intense, is a good example:

Example 12. *Sonata 33 in C Minor, Andante con moto*,
Bars 31-39

The finale of the *C-Minor Sonata* is cast in one of Haydn's unusual hybrid forms, combining elements of sonata-allegro, rondo and variation. Its dark mood and dramatic, rhetorical style match the Sturm and Dräng extremes of the other movements, and its pianistic brilliance is the most highly developed thus far.[9]

With the proper understanding of Haydn's purposes in the *C-Minor Sonata*, its performance can be extremely rewarding to both player and listener.

Reaction and Conflict

In eighteen more sonatas written during the 1770's, there is an unevenness of style. A return to galant levity and frivolity in many of the fast movements, and the inclusion of the minuet in eleven of the works (it had been absent in all five Sturm und Dräng Sonatas), signals at least a partial reaction to past romantic excesses. In four of these Sonatas all three movements are in the same key, as in the very early divertimenti.

But in spite of the reaction, Haydn could not totally discard his romantic ideals. The legacy of the expressive slow movement, for example, persists in eleven of the 1770's works, although none of these is as highly developed or as deeply moving as those in *Sonatas 31* and *33*. And although they are not lyrical as a general rule, the first movements of eleven of the Sonatas of the period retain the moderate tempi that had accommodated such expressiveness in the Sturm und Dräng works. In a number of cases, however, the tempo seems chosen to insure the clarity of rococo articulation, complex ornamentation, or rapid passagework, rather than to enhance lyricism. The first movement of *Sonata 38 in F Major* (H. 23) is a case in point:

Example 13. *Sonata 38 in F Major, Moderato*, Bars 1-9

An occasional *deja vu* of earlier improvizational methods, such as this really amazing passage from the development section of the same movement, serves to reinforce the notion that Haydn's flair for the romantic could not be suppressed:

Example 14. *Sonata 38 in F Major*, Opening Movement, Bars 69-78

The extended, Chopinesque ornament in the slow movement of the next Sonata is even more improvisational:

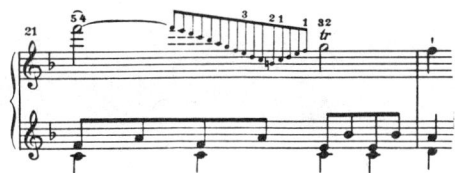

Example 15. *Sonata 39 in D Major* (H. 24), *Adagio*, Bars 21-22

In spite of stylistic conflicts, Haydn made great progress during this period in the synthesis, concentration and balance of formal procedures and in the development of new, completely original ideas. The skill of his craftsmanship increased greatly, particularly in counterpoint, which he pursued at times with academic fervor. In both the *Minuet* and *Trio* of *Sonata 41 in A Major* (H. 26), for example, the second section of the binary form is the exact retrograde of the first.

Example 16. *Sonata 41 in A Major, Menuet and Trio*

In the Sonata preceding this one, *No. 40 in E-Flat Major* (H. 25), the entire *Tempo di Menuet* (here, a finale) is a ternary form written in strict canon!

The eleven minuets in the 1770's Sonatas (six middle movements and five finales) exhibit an increasingly refined stylization and, toward the end of the period, a new kind of classical expressiveness that is sheer listening pleasure. Departures from the traditional minuet forms, in addition to the contrapuntal types shown, include theme and variations in two cases: *Sonatas 44 in F Major* (H. 29) and *45 in A Major* (H. 30).

Sonata 42 in G Major (H. 27), written in 1776, summarizes the reactionary aspect of Haydn's methods and goals in the 1770's perhaps more than any other work of the decade. All three of its movements are in G Major, with no lyrical slow movement. The work is so carefree as to reflect nothing but sunshine. A look at just the opening themes of the three movements is enough to show what a "Pollyanna" effect Haydn must have had in mind:

(a)   First Movement, Bars 1-8

(b)   Second Movement, Bars 1-4

(c)   *Finale*, Bars 1-8

Example 17. *Sonata 42 in G Major*

Taking barely more than ten minutes to perform, this Sonata is a delight for both player and listener. The thematic structures are extremely concise, with little or no filler and no rhetorical or improvisational digressions. The sonata-allegro form of the first movement is "depressurized" by a short development that is not particularly dramatic. The *Minuet*, acting as a kind of slow movement, is typical of the highly stylized type of the period, leaving the ballroom dance far behind.

The finale of the *G Major Sonata* deserves special attention because of the irregular form and experimental nature of its variation technique. It typifies the originality and adventurousness of Haydn's writing during the 1770's, and foreshadows even more bold things to come. (The discussions of this movement and two others below, in *Sonata Nos. 53 and 58*, are best followed if the complete scores are available to the reader.)

The little ternary theme of the finale of the *G-Major Sonata* is unified by the rhythmic relationship of its contrasting parts (bars 1-16). The first two variations (bars 25-72) are fairly standard, but the third (bars 78-104) makes a sudden shift to binary form, with a rondo-like, exact restatement of the first section, followed by a written-out repeat as a further variation in the minor mode. The fourth and last variation (bars 105-52) returns to the ternary plan, but continues the rondo idea of the theme refrain. Repeats of both sections of the theme are then written out as further variations. Haydn was having fun with the form here, and the digression serves to enhance the wit and charm of the movement.

Just as the *D-Major Sonata, No. 30*, was cited as the most balanced of the Sturm und Dräng Sonatas, so does *Sonata 46 in E Major* (H. 31) qualify as the most well-designed and gratifying of the post-Sturm and Dräng period. Written in the same year as the little *G Major Sonata* (1776), the *E Major* sorts out the stylistic conflicts that seem to have plagued Haydn for almost a decade. There are no excesses in this work, but neither is there a lack of depth. It is a synthesis of romantic and rococo ideals, and a fine example of Haydn's craft in the economy and unification of thematic materials. Although the conciseness of the Sonata makes its length barely more than ten minutes, it contains the variety of moods and tonal breadth one expects in a sonata of much larger scope.

In the first movement of the *E-Major Sonata*, gallant, ornamental passagework persists, but here it is infused with a serious, emotional character. The movement is reminiscent both of Haydn's earlier *Sonata in A-Flat*, (No. 31), discussed above, and of some of Mozart's "singing allegros":

Example 18. *Sonata 46 in E Major*, First Movement, Bars 1-8

The development section of this movement is short, though concisely dramatic, and the writing throughout utterly pianistic.

The second movement, with the unusual tempo marking *Allegretto*, is a simple ABA "intermezzo" in the tonic minor, connected to the finale via the V^7 chord. Haydn connected movements in six of his sonatas, including all three movements in *Sonata 45 in A Major* (H. 30). (Beethoven appears to have followed Haydn's lead in this respect some years later.) The *Allegretto* in the *E-Major Sonata* is set in three-voice counterpoint (comparing with the *A-Flat Sonata* discussed above) with the middle section almost totally imitative.

The playful variations that constitute the finale of the *E-Major Sonata* remind us how unpredictable Haydn is. The "a" section of the binary theme cadences surprisingly on the mediant minor (g#) in bar 8:

Example 19. *Sonata 46 in E Major*, Finale, Bars 1-8

The episodic third variation, maintaining only the phrase structure of the theme, is an outburst in the tonic minor, underlining once again that the Sturm and Dräng has not been entirely forgotten:

Example 20. *Sonata 46 in E Major*, Finale, Bars 49-56

The last sonatas of the 1770's achieve even further degrees of both formal and emotional balance. Among these five works, the *Sonata in B Minor, No. 47* (H. 32) stands out as predominately dramatic and moody. Its pianism is the most brilliant and vigorous of any work since the *C-Minor Sonata* of 1771, and it displays vividly Haydn's increasing skill and dramatic sense in the control and elaboration of thematic materials. All three movements have some degree of contrapuntal texture, and the harmony is rich and colorful.

In the first movement of the *B-Minor Sonata*, developmental techniques rival those of Beethoven. A simple three-note dotted motive:

from the second bar of the first theme is fragmented to form a dramatic and suspenseful return at the end of the development section, with more than 30 repetitions and an amazing variety of harmonic colors:

Example 21. *Sonata 47 in B Minor*, First Movement
Bars 39-49

The second movement, a charming *Minuet* with a darker, more agitated *Trio*, functions as a relief between the other two. It carries stylization one step beyond the minuets in previous works and balances the Sonata beautifully.

As in earlier Sonatas where the finale sustains rather than relieves the tension (for example, in *Sonata 31 in A-Flat*), the *Finale* of the *B-Minor Sonata* is in dramatic sonata-allegro form. Its rhythmic drive and energy add to the effect, and its imitative counterpoint is so tightly woven as to sound almost canonic:

Example 22. *Sonata 47 in B Minor, Finale,* Bars 1-15

Cyclically-related motives in all three movements serve to further unify the Sonata. The turn motive, both in ornamental signs (∽) and in the large notes of the opening theme in the first movement (Example 23a), shows up as important thematic material in the *Menuet* and, in inverted form, as a right-hand ostinato accompaniment to the theme in the second section of the Trio. The same inverted motive is found once again in the second section of the *Finale*:

(a) Opening Movement, Bars 1-6

(b) *Minuet*

Bars 6-7   Bars 15-16

(c) *Trio*, Bars 31-32

(d) *Finale*, Bars 39-43

Example 23. *Sonata 47 in B Minor, Finale,*
Bars 1-6

The *Sonata in B Minor* is perhaps the most accomplished in craftsmanship of all the Sonatas Haydn produced in the 1770's. Its outstanding dramatic and pianistic appeal also make it the most outstanding work of the decade.

Sonata 49 in C-Sharp Minor (H. 36) is another one of Haydn's unconventional, unpredictable exercises in the layout and character of its movements. It has some of the unevenness of his earlier, less mature work, but its moods and style have a remarkable range, and its thematic structure a masterful conciseness and unity. The choice of key alone is noteworthy, and its three movements -- *Moderato, Scherzando* and *Menuet and Trio* -- are an attractive formal departure from the norm.

As in the *B-Minor Sonata*, the Sturm und Dräng resurfaces in the *C-Sharp Minor*, with the first movement full of pathos and tension. The sonata-allegro form of this movement is extremely compact, with the first and second themes closely related. The second theme is omitted in the recapitulation, probably because it would be redundant there in the absence of tonal contrast. The development offers rich harmonic textures and remote modulations.

The *Scherzando* heading for the second movement of the *C-Sharp Minor Sonata* refers only to its jocular character, a common application in music of the early Classical period.[10] It is actually a set of variations in 2/4 time, with an alternating major-minor theme, original and inventive in layout. The "a" and "b" sections within each of the two themes are rhythmically and motivicly related, contrasting only in tonality and developmental elaboration:

Example 24. *Sonata 49 in C-Sharp Minor, Scherzando,*
Bars 1-27

The minor theme seems almost a parody of Sturm und Dräng pathos, appearing as is does abruptly after the totally light-hearted major theme. Each of the three variations that follow contains both the major and minor themes, and each is preceded by an exact restatement of the first four bars of the major theme -- a typical example of Haydn's rondo-variation form. (The major theme is the same as that used in *Sonata 52 in G Major* [H. 39] of the same year, an intentional duplication designed by Haydn to show different methods of working out the same material.[11])

The somber and melancholy *Menuet*, one of very few in the minor mode, has none of the ballroom gaiety or elegance of many other minuets of the period, but more of the rustic Austrian folk element found in Haydn's *German Dances* and in some of his symphonic minuets. Its "moderato" heading is the only instance of an actual tempo indication (other than "tempo di menuet") for a minuet in the sonatas. Because of the minor mode of the *Minuet*, the traditional major-minor sequence of the *Menuet* and *Trio* is reversed, with the more lyrical trio in the tonic major (seven sharps!).

Sonatas 48 in C Major (H. 35) and *50 in D Major* (H. 37) are so well-known, at least in pedagogical circles, that their detailed discussion here hardly seems necessary. The best and most popular of the two, the D Major, is discussed in Chapter III in connection with pedagogy, as is the finale of the C Major. The first movement of the latter offers far less variety and originality than most of the sonata movements already discussed here. Its incessant, almost boring triplets in the left hand make unreasonable demands on the young student, to whom it is too often assigned. However, both the slow movement and the popular little rondo finale are beautifully proportioned and well worth study and performance.

Stylistic Maturity: Craft, Humor and Eloquence

In the 1780's Haydn produced seven more piano sonatas (Nos. 52-58) in which he resolved the stylistic conflicts of the past almost completely. The synthesizing process began in the earlier *Sonata 46 in E Major* (Example 18) reached its zenith in this period, in which there is further perfection of formal conciseness and thematic unification, balanced with highly individualistic, personal expression.

Four of the 1780's Sonatas have only two movements. Mono-thematic structures, or closely-related themes, are so frequent as to be almost the rule. With sharply-honed craft and mature expressiveness, Haydn seemed able to produce sonatas in any character or style he chose during this period.

Sturm und Dräng emotionalism is no longer unbalanced or extreme, as it may have been 15 years earlier, but absorbed in the Sonatas with real artistry. The well-known *E Minor Sonata, No. 53* (H. 34), is a masterful example of this. With equal skill and balance, however, Haydn could turn to the objectivity and precision of contrapuntal techniques when they suited his purposes, as in the finales of the *Sonatas in B-Flat Major*, No. 55 (H. 41) and *D Major*, No. 56 (H. 42). Humor, at times satirical and at others just plain fun-loving, becomes an integral part of the structures.

An examination of a number of these sonata movements reveals the range and variety of Haydn's compositional methods during the 1780's. The second work of the period, the aforementioned *E Minor Sonata*, is the most highly-developed. Its opening movement is extremely moody and full or rhythmic energy, with a wide swing of emotions, from anger to exuberant joy. The two principal motives of the movement are set contrapuntally in the two hands, creating a kind of personal dialogue (similar to the opening movement of Beethoven's *Quartet in A Major*, Op. 18, No. 5):

Example 25. *Sonata 53 in E Minor*, Opening Movement, Bars 1-5

The second theme is based primarily on the right-hand character of the principal theme section, once again skillfully condensing the thematic material.

Example 26. *Sonata 53 in E Minor*, Opening Movement, Bars 30-35

The development, based mostly on the principal theme idea, turns the "bouncy" left-hand character into a sostenuto harmonic sequence (briefly suggested in bars 16-18 of the exposition), leading from the submediant (C Major) to the minor dominant (B Minor) with extremely colorful effect:

Example 27. *Sonata 53 in E Minor*, Opening Movement, Bars 46-63

At the end of the development section the hands reverse roles, as if both characters can argue either point, in the manner of a scholastic debate:

Example 28. *Sonata 53 in E Minor*, Opening Movement, Bars 71-78

In the *Adagio* of this Sonata there is throughout a suggestion of the Baroque motivic play prevelant in Haydn's very early rococo works. Yet the fragmentary structure somehow seems to congeal into broad, lyrical phrases. The form is a scaled-down sonata-allegro, with a florid, fantasia-like development section unlike any earlier passage in the Sonatas (with the possible exception of the development section in the opening movement of *Sonata 38 in F Major*, Example 14 above):

Example 29. *Sonata 53 in E Minor, Adagio,*
Development Section

The "attaca subito" indication at the end of the *Adagio* is the earliest incidence of Haydn's actual notation of the connection of movements in the Sonatas. (In *Sonata 46 in E Major* the connection is merely implied by the closing dominant chord.)

The sub-heading of the finale of the *E-Minor Sonata* is an example of the personal expressiveness that was becoming increasingly common in Haydn's works. The term used here, "innocentemente" (innocently), specifically qualifies the stylistic interpretation of the movement. The principal heading, *Vivace molto*, coupled with the dark mood of the opening theme and the somewhat melancholy nature of the second section, might lead the interpreter in a dramatic direction, but "innocence" may well imply a more coquettish and playful rendition. After all, the dramatic depth of the first movement and the fantasia-like *Adagio* need something special to balance them. Haydn, with a characteristic sense of proportion, knew exactly what he wanted. (In the next Sonata, *No. 54 in G Major* [H. 40], the first movement is headed *Allegreto innocente*. The obviously coquettish nature of this movement might confirm, by way of comparison, a similar, though less obvious, interpretation for the E Minor finale, which is the only other movement in the Sonatas where Haydn referred to "innocence.")

To bring out these interpretative ideas, the finale of the *E-Minor Sonata* should be taken somewhat more slowly than is immediately apparent, with the *Vivace molto* idea applying only to the liveliness of the accentuation and the clarity of articulation. A further justification for a more moderate tempo for the finale is its contrast to the opening *Presto* first movement, which should be performed as quickly as possible.

Some playfulness in the rhythm, such as the prolongation of the "sighing" seventh in bar 10, also seems consistent with the satire in Haydn's claim to "innocence":

Example 30. *Sonata 53 in E Minor* Finale, Bars 9-10

The form of the *E-Minor Sonata* finale deserves detailed attention because it is so charmingly original and concise. In an intriguing hybrid of variation and rondo forms, the two-part theme juxtaposes the major and minor modes. The theme is lengthy, but everything grows out of the initial motive in the first two bars. There are the usual ternary sub-sections and key changes, but a subtle form of variation technique is already taking place in this "quasi-exposition" (bars 1-40).

The following two sections (bars 41-100) are basically a repeat of the exposition, with some sub-sections varied and others not. First the minor portion of the theme is restated exactly (bars 41-58), but without notated repeat signs for the subsections. We then suddenly find ourselves in variation form again, with a written-out repeat of the second sub-section varied in melodic ornamentation, harmony and length (bars 59-76). In the next E Major portion of the theme (bars 77-100), the restatement is varied throughout, with the second sub-section extended in length but intact harmonically.

A second restatement of the E Minor portion, again featuring a mixture of exact and varied repetitions, closes the movement (bars 101-36). The E Major portion is not restated a second time, resulting in an A-B-A-B-A scheme completely unified by motivic structure, but with ingenious contrasts in tonality and melodic ornamentation. The exact repetition of the opening eight bars (i.e., the minor theme) at the beginning of each restatement also gives a distinct rondo flavor to the movement (as in the *Scherzando* movement of the *C-Sharp Minor Sonata*, No. 49).

The deservedly popular *E-Minor Sonata* is perhaps the most outstanding example of Haydn's craft in the 1780's. Its bold originality of design, balanced blend of styles and extremely concise structure, as well as its wide range of personal expressiveness, give it the stamp of a masterpiece.

Each of the next three Sonatas (Nos. 54-56, H. 40-42) has only two movements. These works, dedicated to the Princess Esterhaza, seems to dwell on contrapuntal techniques, with further application of mono-thematic design and condensation of structure. The most amazing movement in this regard is the finale of *Sonata 55 in B-Flat Major* (H. 41). The two-voice counterpoint of the theme here is inverted at bar 17, an example of the concentrated craftsmanship in Haydn's working methods:

(a) Opening Theme, Bars 1-5

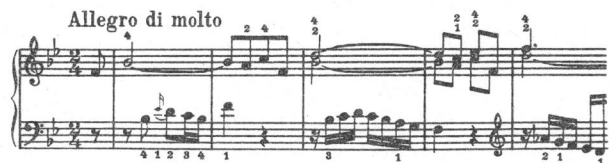

(b) Return, Bars 17-21

Example 31. *Sonata 55 in B-Flat Major*, Finale

The form of this movement is a mixture of several types, put together with total coherence and the rejection of standard procedures that by then was a Haydn hallmark. There are elements of sonata-rondo and variation (as in some earlier works), but with such close thematic relationships throughout as to defy any traditional formal definition.

The ternary theme is followed by a quasi-development section (bars 31-61). Then the restatement features the repeats of the thematic subsections written out as variations (bars 62-121). (Writing out repeats as variations was an earlier procedure of Haydn's, as in the finale of *Sonata 42 in G Major*, analyzed above.) Taking barely three minutes to perform, this movement is the most concentrated of Haydn's contrapuntal keyboard works.

Sonata 58 in C Major (H. 48), also in two movements, is the last one completed in the 1780's. Continuing Haydn's departure from the norm, the first movement is an *Andante* in a totally non-standard form. Further, the finale is another unique structure resembling sonata-rondo. Two eminent Haydn scholars, Karl Geirenger and H. C. Robbins Landon, almost ignore this Sonata, Geirenger dismissing it as "insignificant".[12] Observations here lead to a different conclusion: that the work is a supreme example of Haydn's craft in the elaboration and unity of tightly-constructed themes, with significant advances in pianism over earlier works.

A detailed analysis of the *Andante* of the *C-Major Sonata* seems essential to understanding the originality and uniqueness of Haydn's working methods. Like the finale of the earlier *E-Minor Sonata*, but on a larger scale and with much greater tonal variety, the C Major *Andante* applies variation technique to the major-minor alternation of two closely-related themes. The difference is in the complexity of layout.

The two themes first appear in a standard ternary design: $|a: ||: b\text{-}a :|$ with "a" the major version and "b" the minor. But the return of "a" is both varied and developed in the opening three-part section. The phrase structure of this section (bars 1-26) is among the most irregular that Haydn had yet employed.

The initial statement of the three-part theme is followed by a lengthy section that is partly episodic and partly developmental, but basically related to the motivic structure of the opening thematic section (bars 27-55). Both harmonic digression and thematic expansion characterize this section. When the three-part theme reappears (bars 56-97), it is in variation form, with the first "a" part not repeated and the following "b-a" part stated exactly and then repeated in variation.

More is yet to come! A real development section ensues (bars 98-120), both fragmenting and expanding the major and minor thematic ideas with dramatic intensity and a wide range of tonal color. Finally, the "a" part of the theme returns by itself, varied once more (bars 121-29), but assuming the harmonic progression of its second appearance in the ternary scheme, and interrupted by a deceptive progression to a diminished seventh (vii^7 of v). A six-bar coda, using an initial motive from the second bar of the movement with much richer harmony, ends the story.

The darker colors of the middle and lower ranges of the piano are employed in this movement with great artistic results, building on earlier techniques found in the *Andante* of *Sonata 30 in D Major* (Example 8 [b]) and other sonatas. The form is so irregular and original as to once again defy any real label. As in some earlier works, it contains elements of sonata, variation and rondo. Its apparently loose construction in terms of thematic layout is offset by the amazing unity of its motives and their imaginative elaboration.

The finale of the *C-Major Sonata* is almost as strikingly original and concise as the *Andante*. It is the only movement of the Sonatas actually marked *Rondo* by Haydn, although it does not really resemble any of the standard rondo forms of the time. The irregular order in which the thematic sections are layed out, together with unexpected tonal excursions, confound (yet again!) standard analysis. There is a central development section of 51 bars in length, but there are many other instances of developmental character in the ways themes are handled. The movement procedes in an entirely unpredictable manner, with practically every note growing out of germ motives contained in the first eight bars. With an unbelievable variety of texture, tonality and melodic design, Haydn takes full advantage of the entire range of keyboard colors and techniques in this movement. Pianistically, it rivals the works of Beethoven's early period.

In spite of the neglect of the *C-Major Sonata* in the writings of biographers and theorists, no pianist who is really familiar with the work could deny its greatness. Distinguished by complete freedom from conventional techniques and forms, it is masterful in the pure abstraction of thematic manipulation, and nearly perfect in the resulting balance and beauty of all of its elements.

Mastery of the Form: The Fruition of a Lifetime Effort

Haydn produced only four more keyboard Sonatas in his lifetime: Numbers 59-62 (H. 49-52), completed during the years 1790 to 1795. The dating of the last three of these, composed during his second London sojourn (1794-95), is somewhat in question. It is possible that *Sonatas 60 and 61* were finished after *No. 62*, but the initial publication of the three works as a set, and the short time-span of their composition, make the question somewhat irrelevant.

The small number of Sonatas in the 1790's may be explained partly by Haydn's preoccupation with other creative endeavors, especially the commissions for new works and the conducting assignments he received during his two London residencies. The twelve "London" Symphonies, the great oratorios, and Masses, the final Quartets, and dozens of lesser compositions occupied him during the last years of his creative life. Also, chamber works involving the keyboard, especially the Piano Trios (19 of which were completed in this period), seems to have drawn more of his attention than previously. However, complete freedom of expression (perhaps enhanced by his departure from the confines of Esterhaza in 1791) and total command of the keyboard idiom, along with the supreme perfection on craft that Haydn had by then achieved, resulted in four Sonatas that were individual masterpieces.

Of the eleven movements comprising the last four Sonatas, eight are put together largely with single thematic ideas, the elaboration and variation of which serve as the basis for contrasting sections. The contrasts often involve only different tonality, rhythmic treatment and/or texture. In the sonata-allegro form of the opening movement of *Sonata 60 in C Major* (H. 50), for example, the principal, transition and subordinate themes are all related, with only the closing theme offering any real departure melodically (as in the first movement of Beethoven's "Appassionata"):

(a) Principal Theme, Bars 1-2

(b) Transition, Bars 20-21

(c) Subordinate Theme, Bars 30-31

Example 32. *Sonata 60 in C Major*, First Movement

In the first movement of *Sonata 59 in E-Flat Major* (H. 49), the two principal motives of the opening theme receive varying degrees of transformation in the subordinate theme section:

(a) Principal Theme, Bars 1-4

(b) Subordinate Theme, Bars 25-30

Example 33.   *Sonata 59 in E-Flat Major*, First Movement

These methods persist in slow movements, as in the *Adagio* of *Sonata 62 in E-Flat Major* (H. 52), where there is no second theme as such, but continual elaboration, variation and expansion of the initial motive in bar 1:

(a) Principal Theme,   Bars 1-4

(b) Bridge ("b") Section, Bars 9-10

(c) Middle, or "Development" Section, Bars 19-20

Example 34. *Sonata 62 in E-Flat Major, Adagio*

Developmental techniques that must have influenced the young Beethoven reach their highest point of dramatic impact in these last Sonatas of Haydn. In both *Sonatas Nos. 59 and 60*, unbelievable tension in the return to the tonic at the end of the development section results from the reiteration of a single, secondary motive taken from a brief appearance in the exposition. There is prolonged delay of tonal resolution, and in each case, when the dominant is finally established, the relief is almost physical:

(a) Exposition, Bars 53-55

(b) Development Section, Bars 108-31

Example 35. *Sonata 59 in E-Flat Major*, First Movement

(a) Exposition, Bar 19

(b) Development Section, Bars 92-101

Example 36. *Sonata 60 in C Major*, First Movement

Counterpoint is by now common to developmental textures in the Sonatas, as in the same two movements excerpted above:

Example 37. *Sonata 59 in E-Flat Major,* First Movement
Development, Bars 65-80

Example 38. *Sonata 60 in C Major,* First Movement
Development, Bars 54-63

Humor, so characteristic of many of Haydn's methods in the 1780's, seems an integral part of the thematic structure in all of the last Sonatas. In addition to the "laughing" theme in the *C-Major Sonata* (Example 32a above), unrestrained humor must have prompted this almost ridiculous closing theme in the first movement of *Sonata 62 in E-Flat Major*:

Example 39. *Sonata 62 in E-Flat Major*, Opening Movement, Bars 27-29

This latter example occurs after a pompous and rhetorical opening theme and its subordinate "cousin" have undergone much dramatic interplay. It is as if Haydn were asking the satirical question, "You're not really taking this seriously, are you?" The laughing notes make it clear that the joke is on us!

Other touches of "structural" humor occur in the first movements of *Sonatas 59 and 60*. In the former work, the motive quoted in Example 35 (a) above is the object. After assigning such importance to this motive as to generate the prolonged and dramatic developmental return shown in the earlier example, Haydn treats it thus in the recapitulation:

Example 40. *Sonata 59 in E-Flat Major*, Opening Movement, Bars 179-83

Since there are no other grace-notes of this character in the entire movement, this seems to be another one of Haydn's delightful ways of poking fun.

In the finale of the *C-Major Sonata*, which is in general character jolly and humorous, Haydn enhances the humor by playing with the tonality in a rather devilish manner. Between two varied repetitions, the theme (the only one, incidentally, the stingy Haydn gave the entire movement) is stated first in the tonic minor, leading one-half step up to the Neapolitan, followed by a rhetorical pause; then an abrupt return to the home key, leading one-half step down to the dominant of the mediant (B Major); then another rhetorical pause asks the silent question: "Why can't he decide which direction to go?" Before the question can be answered, surprise! Haydn confirms that he wasn't really going anywhere, with another abrupt return to the tonic and a complete restatement of the varied theme:

Example 41. *Sonata 60 in C Major*, Finale, Bars 88-95

In the last *Sonata in E-Flat Major*, No. 62, Haydn abandons conventional procedures of tonality to the most radical degree of any of his works. In some respects this rhetorical, loosely-constructed work is not really as gratifying as the others. Haydn seems to be overtaken again, late in life, by the Sturm und Drang excesses of his youth. Nonetheless, the brilliant pianism, such as this passage from the first movement, is unmatched in earlier works, and perhaps is the reason why the Sonata is the one most frequently selected by concert artists:

Example 42. *Sonata 62 in E-Flat Major,*
First Movement, Bars 61-57

At the beginning of the development section in the first movement, the rapid progression from B-Flat to C Major leaves little time for preparation, and creates a rhapsodic, fantasia-like atmosphere. The effect is extremely colorful:

Example 43. *Sonata 62 in E-Flat Major*
First Movement, Bars 44-46

There is literally no tonal preparation, after a half-cadence on the dominant of C Minor, for the deceptive entry of the closing theme in E Major near the end of the development in this movement:

Example 44. *Sonata 62 in E-Flat Major*,
First Movement, Bars 65-69

The E Major tonality here foreshadows that of the succeeding *Adagio* movement. (Haydn's total disregard for convention in writing two successive movements in tonalities one-half step apart anticipates the future, while at the same time underscoring his extreme independence.) The *Adagio* is also the most flambouyant, in terms of improvizational character, of all of Haydn's sonata movements of this type. The final statement of the theme, for example, is downright Chopinesque:

Example 45. *Sonata 62 in E-Flat Major, Adagio*, Bars 45-50

The finale of *Sonata 62*, in direct opposition to the other two movements, is dry and tightly constructed. Its intense sonata-allegro form features pianistic techniques far more advanced than in works of just a few years earlier, as in this section of scalar and arpeggiated passage-work:

Example 46. *Sonata 62 in E-Flat Major*, Finale, Bars 131-173

Because of the slow harmonic rhythm, the *Presto* tempo of this movement is best taken near the top of the metronome, rendering the passage nearly as brilliant pianistically as some of Beethoven's early *Sonatas and Piano Trios*, written around the same time.

Sonata 61 in D Major (H. 51) is another slow-fast two-movement work like the C Major, No. 58, discussed above. However, the *Andante* of No. 61 is much more conventional, with less contrast. The prevailing homophonic texture in both movements, together with drawn-out melodic repetitions and the relatively low level of developmental intensity, have led some to label the work Haydn's "Schubertian" Sonata. It is certainly not programmed as frequently as the other three Sonatas from Haydn's late period, but it is nevertheless worthy of study and performance.

The really consummate masterpieces of Haydn's final period are the two Sonatas already discussed in some detail, those in *E-Flat Major, No. 59,* and *C Major, No. 60*. This writer would select the former of these as the best of all, though many would disagree. The slow movements of both works are among the most beautiful utterances to come from Haydn's pen, and the aesthetic balance of each Sonata as a whole is pure poetry. But the E-Flat is generally more lyrical and more of a summation of everything Haydn achieved with the sonata during the previous 30-35 years. It touches the soul, the mind and the body in ways no other of his keyboard works does. It compares with the *104th Symphony* or the *Opus 76 String Quartets* in sheer artistic worth.

Chapter III

Teaching the Sonatas: Rewards and Problems
Selecting A Teaching Edition

Much of the keyboard music of the eighteenth century was written down without indications for articulation, dynamics and accentuation. Printed editions, particularly in the late nineteenth and early twentieth centuries, attempted to assist musicians who lacked knowledge of eighteenth-century style and practice by adding detailed interpretative markings. Unfortunately, too many of these were based on nineteenth-century tastes and often were woefully inaccurate in the stylistic details of eighteenth-century performance practice.

It is therefore important for teachers to obtain, if possible, reliable urtexts for all eighteenth-century music to be taught. Considerable knowledge of eighteenth-century performance practice is essential for correct, "on-the-spot" editing of interpretative markings and ornament realizations to guide the student. But this is not an impossible task for the teacher, and as the student approaches the advanced stage, he/she, too, should be trained to judge the correct manner of performance. There are many aids available to the teacher for this purpose, including prefaces to good urtext editions and other study guides in the form of books and articles.

The best urtext of Haydn's Sonatas is the Universal Edition, the text used by the present writer. The Henle edition (edited by Georg Feder) is almost equally as valuable. Both of these have instructive and helpful prefaces relative to the interpretation of eighteenth-century keyboard music and of Haydn in particular.

Edited publications of the Sonatas which provide some degree of accuracy in eighteenth-century practice for inexperienced students are the Hungarian Edito Musico, edited by Lajos Hernadi and available through Boosey and Hawkes, and the C. F. Peters edition, edited by Martienssen. (These, as well as others mentioned, are listed in the *Bibliography* and discussed in Chapter I in further detail.)

In addition, Willard Palmer's edition of six early Sonatas (Numbers 1, 2, 3, 5, 6 and 9), entitled *Six Sonatinas* and published by Alfred, provides a small and inexpensive volume of teaching material with helpful and fairly stylistic additions of articulation, dynamics and ornament realizations. Fainter print distinguishes Palmer's added markings from those contained in the manuscripts and other early sources. His prefatory explanation of interpretative matters is also useful.

Owning both a well-edited score of the Sonatas and a good urtext for cross-reference is well worth the expense for the really serious study of Haydn.

The Young and Inexperienced Student

For the very young piano student, most of the traditional sonatinas by Clementi, Kuhlau, Dussek and others are too difficult or too long and repetitious, belonging more to the intermediate literature. Also, eighteenth- and nineteenth-century sonatinas are often lacking in expressive quality while making considerable demands in rapid scale work and broken-chord techniques. (Beethoven's Sonatinas are generally an exception, however, and most of Dussek's are more imaginative and romantic than those of his contempories.)

This is not to imply that sonatinas should not be studied at all, but that as an alternative, Haydn's early Sonatas offer a greater variety of high-quality, multi-movement works than can serve as a real training ground for the mature Classical-era sonatas by Mozart, Beethoven, Schubert and Haydn himself. Compared to most sonatinas of the era, Haydn's works provide more rhythmic vitality and imagination, a far broader range of expressive character, certainly more harmonic coloring, and greater formal variety relating directly to sonata style. Music that can boast all this and yet make modest technical demands is rare indeed!

Precise grading of Haydn's Sonatas is inadvisable because of the distinct individuality of each work. Their range of difficulty as a whole accommodates all ages of students: from the inexperienced pre-teen to the more mature high-school and college pianist. For the very young student, the three sonatas in G Major, Numbers 1, 4, and 5 (H. 8, G1 and 11 respectively) are all excellent choices, possessing most of the attributes of the Classical sonata in miniature.

The Problem of Ornamentation

If ornamentation is too complex for a particular student, there is no reason to eliminate a sonata from study for this reason alone. Many ornaments were added in first editions or manuscript copies of Haydn, and others were omitted. It is well-known that ornamentation was partly an improvisational art in the eighteenth century, and selective omission of certain ornaments in the interest of successful study of an entire work usually does not detract from its overall worth. For example, if one performs this opening line of *Sonata 8 in A Major* (H. 5) without ornaments, its basic structure and character are still intact, particularly on the modern piano, which easily can sustain the melodic tone of the eighth-notes:

Example 47. *Sonata 8 in A Major*, Opening Movement, Bars 1-6

Sonata 1 in G Major

The first sonata, whose first-movement exposition is quoted above in Example 4 (Chapter II, page 10), contains all four types of movements found in the usual Viennese Classical sonata. In the embrionic sonata-allegro form of the first movement, the standard sections and key changes are packed into

44 bars without too many complexities. The rapid finger-work required is well within the capabilities of a small, dextrous hand. Rhythmic problems in passages which alternate duple and triple subdivisions are not formidable, but provide excellent training for the greater variety and complexity of rhythm that surely will be encountered in later compositions and in later years of study.

The sixteen-bar *Menuet* of *Sonata 1* is a compact little binary form with no trio, and the *Andante* introduces in a modest way the expressive slow movement so frequently encountered in the Classical sonata. The counterpoint here is an elementary exercise for a kind of texture the student will be faced with later in the mature slow movements of the Viennese Classical masters:

Example 48. *Sonata 1 in G Major*, Slow Movement, Bars 1-4

The finale of this Sonata introduces the student, again in miniature, to the dance-like style, form and rapid tempo common to the majority of sonata finales in the Classical literature.

The usefulness of Haydn's first Sonata as a teaching piece is further enhanced by the limitation of ornaments to long and short trills in only the first two movements. The pedagogical warning that inexperienced students should not be faced with complex, excessive ornamentation, but introduced only gradually to the problem, is well-served by this work.

Sonata 1 makes demands that are not unreasonable for the young student, while at the same time providing a miniature version of the design from which the typical multi-movement sonata of the Classical Era derives its beauty of proportion and balance. The only thing missing is key change among the movements, but there is much more of Haydn to explore in this regard!

Sonata 4 in G Major

The movements of *Sonata 4* are a little larger in scope than those of No. 1, and there is no slow movement as such. The first movement, requiring a little more finger technique and rhythmic control, has a much more extended development section (quoted in Example 5, Chapter II), carrying the student one step closer to the dramatic sonata style of later works. The playfulness in the rhythm of the movement is fun to hear and at the same time tricky to perform. It should both challenge and reward the diligent student.

The *Menuet* includes a *Trio* of contrasting character and key, excellent as a preliminary study of that particular idiom in Viennese sonatas in general. Also, since the *Menuet* acts as a relief between two rapid movements, its speed should be tempered to achieve the proper balance and proportion, acting as a kind of slow movement. It is never too early for students to learn the importance of these artistic considerations, and Haydn offers a variety of such opportunities in a number of very approachable works.

The finale of *Sonata 4*, another ABA dance form, has a contrasting middle section in the tonic minor, providing an opportunity for some expressive interpretation in a rapid tempo (Presto).

Ornamentation in the Sonata as a whole is more complex than in the first Sonata, especially in the second and third movements. But, like the development section of the first movement, this should serve as another step in the learning process. The upper- and principal-note trills are neither voluminous nor insurmountable, and the turn (∾), introduced in the *Trio* and continued in the "B" section of the finale, is a tasteful decoration of the melodic line that can be reasonably negotiated. The first line of the *Trio*, containing three turns, one long approggiatura and one short trill, might be an excellent beginning exercise for eighteenth-century ornamentation:

Example 49. *Sonata 4 in G Major, Trio*, Bars 23-30

Sonata 5 in G Major

The first movement of this work is identical with the finale of the previous sonata.[13] The dance style of the movement is not typical of sonata opening movements in general, but the entire work is worth study, if only because of the pedagogical and aesthetic value of the *Andante*. This lyrical, expressive slow movement in the minor mode provides another large step in the preparatory process for the mature Viennese sonata idiom. It is much larger in scope than the little *Andante* included in the first Sonata, and should be attempted only by those with some previous experience with the less intense and shorter slow movements. For young students, it is a difficult task just to sustain and unify the long melodic phrases, such as that spanning bars 10-18 in the opening section:

Example 50. *Sonata in G Major, Andante*, Bars 1-20

This phrase is followed by a related three-bar extension (bars 18-20) adding even greater breadth to the whole.

The finale of *Sonata 5* is a *Menuet* with a more intense and dramatic *Trio* in the relative minor. Discovering the means by which to achieve the contrasts of mood and emotion called for here (as in the development sections of sonata-allegro forms, also) should be a primary goal of the serious student.

Again, in a work of modest technical demands, Haydn offers in the fifth Sonata more than one exercise, not in pedantic scales and arpeggios, but in the real meaning of sonata style. Dealing with the abstraction in these terms is something not every student can do, but it is also something too many talented students are never given the opportunity to attempt!

Sonata 6 in C Major (H. 10)

This work, comparing in difficulty and types of movements with the *G-Major Sonata*, No. 4, may be even more valuable as an early teaching piece. The *Menuet* acts here as a slow movement (as in the fourth Sonata), with the *Trio* in the tonic, rather than relative, minor. This tonal relationship is common to the minuets found in much of the sonata, chamber and symphonic literature of the period. The *Trio*, as in earlier cases in Haydn, demands a change of mood, but its brevity and textural simplicity lend themselves well to the young pianist.

The *Menuet* is an excellent training piece in two other ways: rhythm and ornamentation. The quarter-note pulse is subdivided by two, three and four units in the short space of the first nine measures -- demanding a rhythmic skill young students must master as soon as possible. Here, within the context of a simple and pleasing musical creation, a straight-forward attack on the problem can be made:

Example 51. *Sonata 6 in C Major, Menuet*, Bars 1-10

Ornamentation in the *Menuet* amounts to a small digest of the different types of upper- and principal-note trills of the eighteenth century. If the student is ready to tackle the technique involved, there is no better place to start. If he/she is not ready, and wishes to concentrate more on the rhythmic problem, ornaments could be omitted (except for the appoggiatura in bar 2, which results in the only sixteenth-note subdivision in the passage).

The finale of *Sonata 6* is of larger scope than those already discussed. It is cast in a small but intense sonata-allegro form, foreshadowing later works in which Haydn, as well as Beethoven, used the finale to sustain rather than relieve the dramatic tension of a sonata. Haydn's introduction of this aesthetic concept in his early Sonatas is a fortunate occurrence for those young students who are able and anxious to progress toward interpretation of the mature sonata literature.

It is obvious that the formal scope, rhythmic complexity and ornamentation of the sixth Sonata are more demanding than in the three G-Major Sonatas discussed earlier, and that its study should not be undertaken by completely inexperienced students. It might therefore be placed more appropriately in the lower range of the intermediate literature.

Teaching Individual Movements

The selection of single movements from Haydn's Sonatas for study or recital repertoire is an excellent idea for those young students who lack the powers of concentration or attention span to undertake an entire work. Some might judge this to be redundant, duplicating, as it were, the many types of single pieces by Haydn, Mozart and Beethoven that are already available. But the way in which a sonata movement functions in a multi-movement cycle, achieving complementary contrast and balance, sets it apart from the separately-composed pieces. As long as the student is made aware of how this works, and how the particular movement he/ she is studying fits into the larger scheme, the learning process is well-served, and some very wonderful music is experienced. In this sense, it is essential that students not only know what the other movements are called and perhaps what their forms are, but also that they have actually heard the entire sonata from which the movement being studied is taken. An ideal procedure would include study and performance of the other movements at a later time.

This sort of instruction goes beyond the motoristic learning of notes, or the casual choice of "something suitable" that may be easily learned for a recital or an audition. It involves the concerted teaching of sonata style and form as an end. If the means of achieving that end vary from studio to studio, it makes little difference, but learning individual movements while understanding their context is one valid approach.

Any of the eleven movements in the four Sonatas discussed above are excellent individually as preparatory material for the different types that function within the sonata cycle. In addition, most of the minuets in the other early Sonatas, through number 9, at least, are comparable in technique and musical value with those already discussed. One other rapid finale, from *Sonata 3 in F Major* (H. 9), is also worthy of separate study.

The Intermediate Student

With a number of years of study behind him/her, the intermediate student can approach some of the more mature Sonatas and individual movements of Haydn with a certain amount of confidence, given the premise that those early years have provided the essential preparatory experience needed for basic understanding of sonata style and technique. The intermediate pianist should be able to handle somewhat more complex ornamentation and a greater variety of rhythm, and to apply the greater powers of concentration required for longer movements.

Also, with the flowering of deeper personal emotions, the intermediate student should begin with some success to project the expressiveness that increasingly evolves in Haydn's work. As with the very young student, Haydn can act as a more musical alternative to the standard sonatinas in this regard. The selection of Haydn is now much broader, and the musical rewards increasingly richer.

Complete Sonatas

A wonderful piece with which to begin is *Sonata 11 in B-Flat Major*

(H. 2). This was discussed in Chapter II (pages 13-15) as an example of the great strides Haydn took toward mature sonata style and form during his early years. Consisting of a *Moderato* opening movement in sonata-allegro form, a beautifully lyrical and rhythmically intricate *Largo* in the relative minor, and a highly stylized *Menuet* and *Trio* as a finale, the *B-Flat Sonata* makes demands on the player that move him/her a great distance toward the full understanding and mastery of Viennese sonata technique and style.

The artful balance Haydn achieved in this work is alone enough justification for time spent in its learning. Studying the *Largo* alone would make the student keenly aware of the vital function of slow movements in the Viennese sonata literature. Preceded in Haydn's Sonatas by only one slow movement approaching its expressive scope and tonal proportions (the *Andante* of *Sonata 5* discussed above), this *Largo* presents a myriad of problems that must be solved if its character is to be accurately portrayed. Yet, the actual pianism is not particularly advanced.

Long singing phrases, such as that in the opening four bars (see Example 2, page 5), need to be unified with the proper dynamic curve and accentuation, and with the right amount of tension and relaxation in the rhythm. The rhythmic freedom implied by the "syncopated rubato" in bar 15 and bars 43-44 must be fully understood. (See the discussion of this technique on page 25.) Also, Rhythmic complexities such as those contained in the following passage have to be carefully negotiated, while at the same time avoiding stiffness:

Example 52. *Sonata 11 in B-Flat Major, Largo*, Bars 12-14

The tonal plan of the *Largo,* within its abridged sonata-allegro form, is richer by far than in any of the movements for younger students discussed earlier. Sustaining the tonal tension of the following passage, for example, is an extremely challenging task:

Example 53. *Sonata 11 in B-Flat Major, Largo,* Bars 29-38

The *Menuet* and *Trio* of the *B-Flat Sonata* presents a musical challenge considerably greater than any in the earlier minuet movements. The individuality and complexity of the rhythm of the opening theme, for example, must be given more than casual attention:

Example 54. *Sonata 11 in B-Flat Major, Menuet*, Bars 1-10

This *Minuet* is stylized to such a degree as to be considered a real instrumental solo rather than a dance, complete with a variety of pianistic textures, including some counterpoint and some rather complicated ornaments and polyrhythms. The key of the *Trio* (B-Flat Minor) is not exactly easy for young students, but luckily its rather sparse texture mollifies the problem.

Three other later Sonatas can be included in the intermediate repertoire: those in *G Major, No. 42* (H. 27), *B-Flat Major, No. 55* (H. 41) and *F Major, No. 57* (H. 47). Each of these is distinctly individual, and includes, as outlined in the discussion of evolution in Haydn's Sonata methods (Chapter II), a number of formal and stylistic innovations. Pianistically, the different movements of these works include finger "show" pieces (the finales of all three), one lyrical slow movement (in No. 57) and a deceiving first movement (also in No. 57) that must be handled with a kind of Schubertian lyricism, lest it sound like a parody of Czerny.

The first of these, *Sonata 42 in G Major*, was labelled "Pollyana" in its outlook (see pages 31-32). If a student ever wishes to have fun with music, this is the piece to assign! The Sonata reverts somewhat to galant ornamentation, which can present some difficulties. Some interestingly problematic fingering patterns crop up in the finale, which demands a very rapid tempo. Also, there is a potential problem of endurance with the extended Alberti bass passages in the first movement. But in spite of all of this, the Sonata is small enough in scope and light enough in texture to allow concentration on solving the problems -- an achievement that should serve the student well for more difficult works.

Sonata 55 in B-Flat Major is the most unusual of the three, having only two movements and, in the finale, one of the most concentrated examples of counterpoint found in all of Haydn (see Example 31, page 49). The movement vividly illustrates the point that Bach's *Inventions* are not the only alternative for the study of contrapuntal technique!

The *F-Major Sonata*, No 57, is probably a combination of an unrelated first movement with the first two movements of *Sonata 19* (not in Hoboken) in a different key.[14] But the resulting three-movement work is a valuable example of variety in the kinds of movements Haydn created, all within the reach of an intermediate technique.

The first movement of the *F-Major Sonata*, as referred to earlier, appears at first glance to be a two-part invention or toccata-like exercise in scales and broken thirds equally divided between the two hands, with little opportunity for expressive treatment:

(a) Bars 1-7

(b) Bars 27-32

Example 55. *Sonata 57 in F Major*, Opening Movement

But Haydn's *Moderato* tempo marking and the gently undulating melodic lines give the clue that this is really a "singing" movement, with the sixteenth-note a kind of melissmatic unit of vocal quality. Such a treatment can result in a richly expressive interpretation, and should add yet another stylistic concept to the student's growing command of sonata repertoire.

The *Adagio* of the *F-Major Sonata* is a lovely arabesque with many of the rhythmic complexities and phrasing problems of a Mozart or Beethoven slow movement. It is fairly short, connecting to the finale with the dominant chord, and its very personal expressiveness demands thoughtful and sensitive interpretation.

There is nothing serious about the last movement of the *F-Major Sonata*, and here it is important for the student to indulge in the gaiety and light-hearted dance style typical of Haydn's finales. To capture the right amount of humor in purely abstract sound is the task at hand (as in the finale of the earlier *Sonata 42*), and a certain sense of abandonment should accompany the effort. Again, a lesson in the balance of sonata movements can be an important result.

Individual Movements

Lyrical slow movements of great beauty and expressiveness are rare in the early "training" literature of the multi-movement genre, except in Haydn's early Sonatas, where such movements are a frequent occurrence. Some of them are pure masterpieces, well within the grasp of a modest technique. What better way to prepare a student for such later studies as, perhaps, the *Adagio* of Beethoven's *C-Minor Sonata*, Opus 10, No. 1, or the *Arioso* of his Opus 110. (Only one or two of the early Mozart Sonatas contain "preparatory" slow movements, such as the *Sonata in F Major*, K. 279, that are equally as valuable and approachable.)

One such movement in Haydn's works is the *Adagio* of *Sonata 13 in G Major* (H. 6). This Sonata, like the earlier and much easier *Sonata 1 in C Major*, contains all four of the standard types of movements found in various combinations in the late eighteenth-century sonata. However, the first movement is too long, complex and difficult for the intermediate student. This is unfortunate, because its rich, chromatic texture is an important example of Haydn's early accomplishments in harmonic language, as in the following passage:

Example 56.
Sonata 13 in G Major,
First Movement, Bars 9-13

But the *Adagio* (third movement) could certainly be studied separately by intermediate students. It is not long (25 bars), and some of the complex ornamentation could be omitted (except the long trills in bars 6-7 and 21-22, which are the only means of sustaining the single note of the top voice). Although somewhat rococo at first glance, the ornamental melodic line exudes lyricism from every one of its many notes, demanding a very slow tempo and extremely sensitive handling of tone and nuance in the long, singing phrases. The left hand joins in the poetry, with a simple, melancholy "solo" beneath the long trills:

Example 57. *Sonata 13 in G Major, Adagio*, Bars 5-8

There are several opportunities for the introduction of rubato where the harmonic tension builds and subsides, as in the following:

Example 58. *Sonata 13 in G Major, Adagio*, Bars 3-4

And the creative exercise of fermata realization, a common eighteenth-century practice, can be introduced to the student in a fairly simple manner, as in the following suggested in the Universal Edition:

Example 59. *Sonata 13 in G Major, Adagio*, Bar 10

This Sonata is the earliest of four in which Haydn implied such improvisation, or "embellishment" (as discussed in Chapter II, page 22). As an encouragement of creativity, students who are so inclined could be challenged to improvise their own realizations.

    There are five other individual moments that can be both useful in technical training and musically rewarding to the intermediate student as rapid "show" pieces: the finales of *Sonatas 15, 30, 50, 53, and 54* (H. 13, 19, 37, 34 and 40). These movements have a wide variety of scope, form and technique suitable for students of varying abilities and powers of concentration.

    The first, the finale of the *E-Major Sonata*, No. 15, features rapid double thirds, brilliant arpeggiation (but never outside one octave), and some troublesome Alberti bass sections that challenge the player to produce a toccata-like sound in a rapid tempo, with crisp clarity and a dance style that is kept light. The movement is in sonata-allegro form, with a development section so concentrated as to use only one three-note motive, fragmented from the first theme, for most of its materials. The student should notice that the left-hand octave accompaniment in bars 56-57, seeming to introduce a completely new mood and texture, is actually an augmentation of the central motive:

Example 60. *Sonata 15 in E Major*, Finale, Bars 44-58

Conveying the proper sense of tension in such passages is a musical skill that must be accomplished sooner or later. For such a purpose, this movement is an excellent place to start.

The next finale, in *Sonata 30 in D Major*, is entirely different. Its form is one of the earliest examples of Haydn's rondo-variation hybrid, an important structural concept for students to understand if they are to tackle his later works. (See the discussion of the *Finale of Sonata 42*, page 32.) Except for some double thirds that are not too difficult, and some Alberti bass in the final variation which taxes the dexterity and endurance of an inexperienced left hand, the texture of the movement consists mostly of two voices in a layout of very pianistic patterns. The rapid finger technique required is certainly not easy, but there are no problems of wide lateral motion or complex tonal structures.

The finale of *Sonata 50 in D Major* is perhaps more well-known among piano teachers and students than any other individual movement of

Haydn. It is designed in a concise, simple rondo form, with little ornamentation and few demands for extensive, rapid finger work. The Alberti bass in the final section could tax the left-hand endurance of young students, and the variety of articulation throughout the movement calls for precision and stylistic understanding. Nevertheless, as an introduction to more complex Haydn, the movement may be the best one with which to begin.

The finale of the well-known *E-Minor Sonata*, No 53, already discussed formally and stylistically at some length (Chapter II, pages 46-48), is perhaps the most difficult of the four because of its more complex key structure and some extended Alberti basses with rapidly changing harmonies. A passage such as the following is bound to be problematic without an accomplished left-hand technique:

Example 61. *Sonata 53 in E Minor*, Finale, Bars 12-18

There are also some problems of rapid and wide lateral shifts, and some troublesome ornamentation. These challenges probably can be met only by the best students, and might therefore place the movement in the advanced category by some standards.

The last of the five finales under consideration -- that of *Sonata 54 in G Major* -- is the most fun and light-hearted. It is predominantly a "right-hand" piece, having only three bars of rapid Alberti bass in a left-hand texture of mostly two-voice, repeated eight-note chords. However, some counterpoint intensifies the physical requirements, as in the following:

Example 62. *Sonata 54 in G Major, Finale*, Bars 25-29

And where the Alberti bass does occur, the student is also saddled with rapid, wide leaps which complicate the learning process:

Example 63. *Sonata 54 in G Major, Finale*, Bars 68-72

But the movement is so gratifying and so much fun, that the intense work it probably requires should be easy to inspire in a talented student.

The finale of *Sonata 48 in C Major* (H. 35), although not particularly a "show" piece, is so typical of "jolly" Haydn, with its rollicking rhythm and folk-dance style, as to attract almost any bright student. The movement is nearly as popular among young piano students as the more showy finale of the *D-Major Sonata* (No. 50), but its technical demands are more modest. The left hand must cope with some tricky fingerings amid rapid, multi-directional dotted rhythms and triplets, but these are relieved for the most part by simple repeated chords in the right hand. Some more complex counterpoint appears with left-hand broken octaves and, subsequently, contrary melodic voices in the two hands, but most of the movement is of sparse texture with plenty of "resting" places. Its form, an irregular simple rondo unified by a single theme in different tonalities (except for the contrasting theme in the short C-minor section) is easily comprehensible to young students. Its performance is usually successful.

The Mature Student

There are at least ten Haydn Sonatas that should be considered major repertoire for the advanced student. A brief listing and description of these is designed for those who wish to investigate them further.

Sonata 30 in D Major (H. 19)

The finale of this Sonata was discussed above as suggested intermediate teaching material, but since the content and scope of the other two movements demand such maturity from the player, study and performance of the work as a whole should be delayed until a later age, or a more advanced stage of development.

The Sonata was also discussed stylistically in Chapter II (pages 16-20) as the most balanced of the five "Sturm und Dräng" Sonatas of Haydn's "romantic" period. The first movement is quite extended in design, with a three-theme exposition covering 42 bars, and a dramatic development section more than half the length of the exposition (see Example 8a, page 18.)

There are problems of tone production and phrase continuity in the first movement, especially in passages containing a mixture of long notes and rapid scales, as in the following:

Example 64. *Sonata 30 in D Major*, First Movement,
Bars 12-13

The wealth of galant ornamentation must be blended into the melodic lines without rhythmic disruption or physical awkwardness:

Example 65. *Sonata 30 in D Major*, First Movement,
Bars 4-8

Also, the development section (Example 8a) requires a certain amount of pianistic brilliance and a distinct sense of the dramatic.

The *Andante* of *Sonata 30*, also featuring a thin, two-voice texture, has a subtle and graceful charm, reinforced by extremely sensitive color contrast of the high and low registers of the piano (see Example 8b, page 19.) The movement calls for a really mature pianist; the notes are easy, the style is not!

Sonata 31 in A-Flat Major (H. 46)

This sonata was also one of the Sturm und Dräng works discussed stylistically in Chapter II (pages 20-22). The examples quoted there should be sufficient to remind the reader of the nature and scope of the Sonata. Even more than in the previous *D-Major Sonata,* the lyricism of the A-Flat work demands mature pianism. The overall technical and aesthetic content of its three movements can result in an extremely attractive and emotionally rewarding performance, provided the student is up to the task.

Sonata 33 in C Minor (H. 20)

Discussed at length in Chapter II (pages 22-26) as the high point of Haydn's romantic period, the *C-Minor Sonata* has a kind of dramatic appeal that should be successful with any audience. The examples shown, along with the discussion of its pianism and stylistic originality, identify the work as important sonata repertoire for the mature pianist.

Sonata 38 in F Major (H. 23)

This work may be the most difficult to balance and in which to achieve enough contrast to render it artistically effective. It is one of those works in Haydn's post-Sturm-und-Dräng period with an unsettled, inconsistent stylistic approach. Except in the brilliantly improvisational development section (quoted in Example 12, page 25), the decorative thirty-second notes in the first movement present a real problem, not only in technical clarity, but also in the creation of contrast. The entire second theme and closing theme portions, comprising more than half the exposition, are an extended "toccata," tending to be more repetitious and harmonically less colorful than Haydn's best works of the period. Yet, a technically clean rendition, with sufficient emphasis on the dramatic shape of the development section, can result in an exciting and gratifying performance. Mastery of the demanding finger work here is absolutely essential:

Example 66. *Sonata 38 in F Major*, Opening Movement, Bars 20-46

The slow movement (*Adagio*) of the *F-Major Sonata* also is not as lyrical as those of the Sturm und Dräng works, leaning more heavily on the galant style. With proper care that the tempo is slow enough to capture the singing quality and dynamic shading of triplet sixteenth-notes, and with sensitive melodic treatment of the abundant ornamental turns, this *Adagio* can serve as a satisfying and balanced contrast between the two outer movements.

The finale, motivically the most repetitious of the three movements, seems to be a somewhat groping, preliminary attempt by Haydn to arrive at the unified, monothematic design that so often distinguishes his later works. If performed rapidly and clearly enough, however, the movement can convey a certain controlled breathlessness that sweeps the listener to a satisfying conclusion of the three-movement cycle.

Sonata 46 in E Major (H. 31)

This work, discussed in Chapter II as the most well-designed of Haydn's post Sturm-und-Dräng, "reactionary" period (see pages 33-35), has a blend of lyricism and galant decoration that the *F-Major Sonata* lacks. All of its movements are more concise, and it avoids the loose kind of repetitiousness of some of the earlier Sonatas of the period.

In the first movement, complex ornamentation and an abundance of scalar passages must be transformed into real melodic structure. Expert voicing of the three-part contrapuntal texture in the middle movement is essential for the proper definition of the thematic ideas. The light-hearted *Presto* finale presents no particular technical problem, except for some tricky fingering of fast notes and perhaps the clarity of short trills (∿). Mastery of the problems in all three movements provides the student with a gratifying piece of repertoire that audiences are bound to find pleasing and graceful.

Sonata 47 in B Minor (H. 32)

If any one of Haydn's sonatas can be singled out as "Beethovenian," at least in spirit, the *B-Minor Sonata* is the most obvious choice. Described at length in Chapter II as the most dramatic and moody of Haydn's post-Strum-und-Dräng period (see pages 36-39), the work should lend great artistic value to any recital program.

A thoughtful interpretation should seek to achieve the balance Haydn intended for the Sonata. The extreme contrast of the *Minuet* with the finale, for example, must be created without triteness, and the compact thematic structure of the entire work should create at the same time a sense of tension and a solid feeling of formal continuity. All this requires musical maturity.

Ornamentation in the first movement, as in the earlier *C-Minor Sonata*, is abundant, yet so much an integral part of the melodic line as to call for a thorough understanding of eighteenth-century style, and experience in the handling of ornaments. Projecting the extreme stylization of the *Minuet* calls for sophistication, and finger technique in the *Presto* finale takes more endurance than at first is apparent.

The *B-Minor Sonata* should be undertaken by students only as a serious, major piece of repertoire, in spite of its relatively short length (about 12-13 minutes).

Sonata 50 in D Major (H. 37)

Overpopularization of this Sonata, like the *C-Sharp Minor Prelude* of

Rachmaninoff or Debussy's *Clair de lune*, should not detract from its intrinsic value in performance and teaching, if two conditions are observed: 1) it is not the only Haydn sonata worth studying, and 2) it should not be attempted by inexperienced students.

The first movement, unfortunately the one most frequently attempted by young students, can be the downfall. Rapid, sixteenth-note counterpoint, multi-directional arpeggiation covering two octaves, complex ornamentation, and extended left-hand passagework are just a few of the problems confronting the player. The movement is among the brightest and most well-composed of those in the Sonatas. Its mastery is extremely rewarding, but this is no small task!

The *Largo*, really a short intermezzo introducing the finale, must be approached with a depth of feeling that by itself attempts to balance the prevailing gaiety of the two, much longer outer movements. The unsettled and dramatic effect of the almost spasmotic rhythm is not effective if marred by the slightest inaccuracy. (The rhythm, and the dark, brooding, almost elegaic character of the movement, are reminiscent of Bach's *E-Flat* Minor *Prelude* from the first volume of the *Well-Tempered Clavier*.) The vast majority of students who attempt the first and/or last movements of the Sonata probably do not even look at the *Largo*, let alone perform it. This may be just as well, since, as already implied, the *Largo* calls for a high degree of maturity.

The finale of the *D-Major Sonata* has a high success rate as a separate study for young (intermediate) students, as discussed above. But performing the complete Sonata is a much different story.

Sonata 53 in E Minor (H. 34)

The finale of the *E-Minor Sonata*, like that of the previous *D-Major Sonata*, was included in the discussion of individual movements suitable for intermediate students. (The style and form of the entire Sonata are also discussed at length in Chapter II, (pages 42-48). Like the D-Major, the first two movements of the *E-Minor Sonata* demand certain technical and interpretative powers beyond the medium level.

The speed of the first movement, with intense "dialogue" between the two hands, necessitates such precision and clarity of finger technique as to defeat a player of lesser accomplishments. Because of the relatively slow harmonic rhythm, the "presto" character cannot be conveyed without a very rapid tempo, making sixteenth-notes in the 6/8 meter move at the rate of about 11 or 12 per second ($\droteq$ = 104-08).

The *Adagio* is another one of those lyrical slow movements that, like so many in Haydn's mature period, cannot be approached by those who lack considerable experience with the particular style involved. The long melodic phrases, decorated in the galant manner by myriads of thirty-second-notes, are too easily fragmented by insensitive or misplaced accentuation, or by a lack of appropriate shading. (see Example 18, page 34.)

Sonata 59 in E-Flat Major (H. 49) and *Sonata 60 in C Major* (H.50)

It was suggested at the end of Chapter II that these two works are the best among all the extant Sonatas of Haydn. Details that have already dealt with their style and form (see pages 52-62) seem sufficient to illuminate their equally superior value as teaching and performing repertoire. In both artistic and technical demands on the performer, and in audience appeal, these two works have to be considered major repertoire along with the best Sonatas of Mozart and Beethoven.

Two Unsuitable Sonatas

Because of their relative popularity in the repertoire, it should be noted that, as advanced teaching material, two particular Sonatas may not be as suitable for study or as successful in performance as is traditionally thought.

Sonata 32 in G Minor (H.44), a two-movement work from Haydn's Strum und Dräng period, is smaller in scope than either of the two which precede it (Numbers 30 and 31, both recommended for mature students), and less satisfying than all four of the other Sonatas from that period. It has no more or no less of the decorative, rococo figuration which seems to persist in these sonatas. But whereas the others balance the decorative element with a deeply emotional lyricism, exploiting the singing powers of the piano, the *G-Minor Sonata* seems more of a harpsichord piece of rather shallow content. It is also the most repetitious in melodic design. Study time might be better spent on any of the numerous other works recommended.

Sonata 62 in E-Flat Major (H. 52) is perhaps the most popular with performing pianists, but its first movement is too-loosely constructed and too radical in form and tonal relationship to result in a convincing performance by any but the most mature artists. The abrupt modulations and lengthy, rhetorical pauses are even more difficult to bridge than in the *C-Minor Sonata* discussed earlier, making continuity a real problem. Pianists still in the student stage are likely to encounter a great deal of frustration in attempting to interpret and effectively perform this movement. However, the other two movements are real gems which merit individual study. (For the stylistic discussion of the entire *Sonata*, see pages 62-67 in Chapter II.)

Chapter IV

Summary and Conclusion

It is evident to this writer that in the forty-year evolution of his keyboard Sonatas, Haydn achieved the goals suggested in Chapter II: to remain flexible and original regarding structure, and to continually expand the emotional substance of his work. In the establishment of formal and stylistic prototypes, his *Symphonies* and *String Quartets* can claim primary importance in their respective genres. Just as importantly, the Sonatas are the basis for Classical form and style in the keyboard literature of major composers up to the present day. They are also works of immortal beauty, capable of lifting the soul and the mind to the exalted plane shared by the *Symphonies* and *Quartets*, albeit on a smaller scale.

This critical study of the stylistic and formal evolution and the pedagogical value of Haydn's Sonatas attempts to reconstruct their importance in the contemporary musical world. It is hoped that teachers and students may be convinced of the value of Haydn's work as solid alternatives to Mozart and Beethoven, and, in the case of his early Sonatas, as valuable alternatives to the traditional sonatinas. It is also hoped that performing artists can begin to give Haydn his due place in the keyboard repertoire, reversing the unjust neglect he has suffered. Thanks to diligent editors like Christa Landon and Georg Feder, and to dedicated scholars like A. P. Brown, William S. Newman, and Jens Peter Larsen, there has been sufficient reconstruction of the music and its historical context to provide Haydn enthusiasts with enough equipment to pick up the scores and start reaping the rewards of an untapped gold mine!

Endnotes

[1] See Christa Landon's *Preface* in Volume I of the Universal Edition (3rd Edition), page XV, referring to the so-called "first edition" of Haydn's keyboard works, published by Breitkopf and Härtel from 1800 to 1806, in which Haydn stated (in the *Foreword*) that he had deleted "those works of my early youth, which are not worth preserving."

[2] The earlier Breitkopf and Härtel edition (1800-06), referred to in endnote 1, included only 34 Sonatas. Landon's *Preface* discusses not only this early publication, but also its source materials.

[3] The Peters Edition was antedated by a four-Volume publication containing 42 Sonatas by Breitkopf and Härtel in 1932, but this was generally less accessible to American buyers.

[4] Also, the manuscripts of the previously unpublished "Raigern Sonatas" (UE Nos. 17 and 18) were first discovered by George Feder in the Raigern Monastery in Moravia in 1961, two years before Christa Landon's Edition first appeared.

[5] See the *Collation* of Haydn Sonata numbers in various editions (*Appendix*, pages 114-15), in which Hoboken and UE numbers can be matched.

[6] See "Haydn's Clavichord and a Sonata Manuscript", by Phillip James, in *The Musical Times*, April 1, 1950, pp. 314-15.

[7] Other slow movements to which this practice applies are those in *Sonata 13 in G Major* (H.6) and *Sonata 52 in G Major* (H39). See Example 59, page 87, for an embellishment of the fermata in Sonata 13 suggested in the Universal Edition.

[8] This was a fairly common way of notating implied rubato in the eighteenth century. See also the *Adagio of Sonata 11 in B-Flat Major* and the *Trio* sections of the *Minuets* in *Sonatas 12 in A Major* (H.12) and *18 in E-Flat Major*.

[9] Claims that this work was the first for piano, rather than harpsichord or clavichord, seem doubtful because of the apparent pianistic idioms in the three or four Sonatas that precede it.

[10] The Beethovenian type of rapid, brilliant 3/4 time "Scherzo" did not really appear until about 1785, in the works of J. M. Kraus.

[11] See Haydn's letter to his publisher, dated April 1780, in which he requested, and received, an "advertisement" with the publication of these Sonatas explaining the intentional duplication, in *The Collected Correspondence and London Notebooks of Joseph Haydn*, ed. H. C. Robbins Landon 25-26.

[12] See *Haydn: A Creative Life in Music*, by Karl Geirenger, p. 305.

[13] See the *Preface* to the Universal Edition, Vol. I, p. XVI, where Christa Landon suggests that *Sonata 5*, numbered as "D-1" among the "Klavierstück" listed in Hoboken's 1957 *Catalogue*, was a combination of three unrelated movements.

[14] See Landon's explanation of the origins and authenticity of this work, P. XVI, Universal Edition *Preface*, Volume I.

Bibliography

Books, Periodicals and Dissertations

(Except for the important Hoboken *Catalogue*, only works in English are listed.)

Adler, Guido. "Haydn and the Viennese Classical School," *Musical Quarterly*, Vol. 18 (1932), pp. 191-207.

Anderson, C. A. "Some Aspects of Melodic Structure and Style in the Early and Middle Keyboard Sonatas of Joseph Haydn," Dissertation Abstracts, Mar., 1971.

Andrews, Harold Lee. "Tonality and Structure in the First Movements of Haydn's Solo Keyboard Sonatas," unpublished dissertation, Chapel Hill, NC, University of North Carolina, 1967.

Aulabaugh, Alan. "An Analytical Study of Performance Problems in the Keyboard Sonatas of F. J. Haydn," unpublished dissertation, Iowa City, IA, University of Iowa, 1958.

Bach, C.P.E. *Essay on the True Art of Playing Keyboard Instruments*, trans. and ed. William J. Mitchell (from the 1752 German publication), New York, W.W. Norton, 1949.

Banowitz, Joseph. "Gould's Remarkable Haydn Series," *Piano Quarterly*, No. 20, (Winter., 1982-83), pp. 9-10.

Brown, A. Peter. *Joseph Haydn's Keyboard: Sources and Style*, Bloomington, IN, Indiana University Press, 1986.

Brown, A. Peter. "Problems of Authenticity of Two Haydn Keyboard Works," *Journal of the American Musicological Society*, Vol. 25, No. 1 (1972), pp. 85-97.

Brown, A. Peter. "A Reintroduction to Joseph Haydn's Keyboard Works," *Piano Quarterly*, Vol. XXI, No. 79 (Fall, 1972), pp 42-47.

Brown, A. Peter. "The Solo and Ensemble Keyboard Sonatas of Joseph Haydn: A Study in Structure and Style," unpublished dissertation, Evanston, IL, Northwestern University, 1971.

Brown, A. Peter. "The Structure of the Exposition in Haydn's Keyboard Sonatas," *Musical Record*, Vol. 36 (1975), pp. 102-09.

Dent, Edward J. "Haydn's Pianoforte Works," *Monthly Musical Record*, Vol. 62 (1932), p. 191-207.

Geirenger, Carl. *Haydn, A Creative Life in Music*, Berkely, CA, University of California Press, 1963, rev., ed., 1966.

Hinson, Maurice. *Guide to the Pianist's Repertoire*, ed. Irwin Freundlich, Bloomington, IN, Indiana University Press, 1973, pp. 307-12.

Hoboken, Anthony van. *Joseph Haydn Thematisch-bibliographisches Werkverzeichnis, Instrumental werke*, Mainz, B. Schotts Söhne, 1957.

Holis, Helen R. *The Musical Instruments of J. Haydn: An Introduction*, Washington, D. C., Smithsonian Institution Press, 1977.

James, Phillip. "*Haydn's Clavichord and a Sonata Manuscript,*" *Musical Times*, Vol 71, No. 1046 (April 1950), pp. 314-16.

Landon, H. C. Robbins. *The Collected Correspondence and London Notebooks of Joseph Haydn*, London, Barrie and Rockliff, 1959.

Landon, H. C. Robbins. "Haydn's Piano Sonatas," *Essays on the Viennese Classical Style*, New York, MacMillan, 1956, pp. 44-67.

Lang, Paul Henry. "Haydn's Sonatas: Both Amiable and Profound," *Hi-Fi/Musical America*, Vol. 28 (June, 1978), pp. 80-82.

Larsen, Jens Peter, Howard Server and James Webster, eds. *Haydn Studies: Proceedings of the International Haydn Conference, Washington D.C., 1975*, New York, W.W. Norton, 1981.

Maxwell, Carolyn, ed. *Haydn, Solo Piano Literature: A Comprehensive Guide, Annotated and Evaluated With Thematics*, Boulder, CO, Maxwell Music Evaluation, 1983.

Mitchell, William J. "The Haydn Sonatas," *Piano Quarterly*, Vol. XV, No. 58 (Winter, 1966-67), pp. 9, 20-23.

Newman, William S. "The Pianism of Haydn, Mozart and Beethoven Compared," *Piano Quarterly*, Vol. XXVII (Spring, 1979), pp. 14-30.

Newman, William S. *The Sonata in the Baroque Era*, rev. ed., Chapel Hill, NC, University of North Carolina Press, 1966.

Newman, William S. *The Sonata in the Classical Era*, Chapel Hill, NC, University of North Carolina Press, 1963.

Parrish, Carl. "Haydn and the Piano," *Journal of the American Musicological Society*, Vol. I, No. 3 (Fall, 1948), pp. 27-34.

Pollack, Carla. "Viennese Solo Keyboard Music, 1740-1770: A Study in the Evolution of Classical Style," unpublished dissertation, Boston, MA, Brandeis University, 1984.

Rath, Edward. "Piano Study in Vienna According to Hans Kann," *Clavier*, Vol. XXI, No. 4 (April, 1982), pp. 16-22.

Rosen, Charles. *The Classical Style: Haydn, Mozart and Beethoven*, New York, W. W. Norton, 1971.

Rothschild, Curt. *Musical Performance in the Times of Mozart and Beethoven*, London, A. & C. Black, 1961.

Shamgar, Beth. "Rhythmic Interplay in the Retransitions of Haydn's Piano Sonatas," *Journal of Musicology*, Vol. III, No. 1 (Winter, 1984), pp. 55-68.

Slenczynska, Ruth. "Follow-Up on Haydn: Sonata for Piano No. 35 in A-Flat Major," *Clavier*, Vol. II, No. 7 (1972), pp. 188-26.

Steiger, Arthur. "Exploring an Early Haydn Sonata," *Clavier*, Vol. XX, No. 5 (May-June, 1981), pp. 15-19.

Tovey, Donald Francis. "Haydn Pianoforte Sonata in E-Flat, No. 1." *Essays in Musical Analysis: Chamber Music*, London, Oxford University Press, 1944, pp. 9105.

Willett, T. E. "A Study of Haydn's Piano Sonatas," unpublished dissertation, Urbana, IL, University of Illinois, 1946.

Editions of Haydn's Sonatas

The Fifty-Two Piano Sonatas, 4 vols., New York, Lea Pocket Scores, 1959 (reprint of the 1918 Breitkopf und Härtel Edition).

Sämtliche Klaviersonaten, 3 vols., ed. Christa Landon, fingering by Oswald Jonas, Vienna, Universal Edition (Vienna Urtext Editions), 1964, 1966, 1973.

Sämtliche Klaviersonaten, 3 vols., ed. Georg Feder, fingering by Hans-Martin Theopold, Munich, G. Henle, 1972.

Sämtliche Sonaten für zu zwei Händen, 4 vols., ed. Hermann Zilcher, Leipzig, Breitkopf und Härtel, 1932.

Sechs leicht Divertimenti, ed. Carl Adolf Martiennsen, New York, C. F. Peters, 1952.

Selected Sonatas in Two Volumes, ed. Lajos Hernadi, New York, Boosey and Hawkes (for Editio Musico, Budapest), n.d.

Six Sonatinas, ed. Willard A. Palmer, Sherman Oaks, CA, Alfred, 1970. (UE Nos. 1, 2, 3, 5, 6, 9)

Sonatas (43), 2 vols, New York, Kalmus, n. d. (Reprint of the same Sonatas in the C. F. Peters Edition of 1937.)

Sonatas (34), 2 vols, New York, Kalmus, n. d. (Reprint of the two-volume G. Schirmer edition of 1894, with 14 additional Sonatas in a second volume. Also corresponds with the 34 Sonatas in the Breitkopf und Härtel "First Edition" of 1800-06.)

Sonatas (20), 2 vols., ed. L. Klee and S. Lebert, New York, G. Schirmer, 1894.

Sonatas for Pianoforte, 2 vols., Philadelphia, Theodore Presser, n.d.

Sonaten für Klavier zu Zwei Händen, 4 vols., ed. Carl A. Martiennsen, New York, C. F. Peters, 1937.

Discography of Haydn's Sonatas

Notes: 1) This discography includes only those artists who have recorded six or more of Haydn's Sonatas.

2) Both currently-available releases and important out-of-print releases are included. Out-of-print records may be available in good music libraries.

3) Recorded performances use the modern piano unless otherwise noted.

Alpenheim, Ilse von. *Complete Sonatas.* Vox SVBX 5490-3 (12 discs).

*Balsam, Artur. *11 Sonatas.* Oiseau-Lyre S273-5 (3 discs). Sonatas 13, 20, 33, 37, 38, 43, 45, 46, 48, 51, 54.

*Balsam, Artur. *2 Sonatas.* Oiseau-Lyre S-136E. Sonatas 18, 22, 26, 46.

Bilson, Malcolm. *7 Sonatas.* Titanic 51/2 (fortepiano). Sonatas 31, 33, 35, 38, 41, 47, 53.

Bilson, Malcolm. *2 Sonatas.* Nonesuch 78018 (fortepiano). Sonatas 59, 62.

Brendel, Alfred. *11 Sonatas.* Phillips 950074: Sonatas 33, 59. Phillips 412228-1PH and 412228-2PH (compact disc): Sonatas 47, 53, 56. Phillips 410045-2PH (compact disc): Sonatas 58, 60, 61. Phillips 416365-PH1: Sonatas 50, 54, 62.

*Buchbinder, Rudolph. *Complete Sonatas*: in Haydn Edition, Vol. IX (Keyboard Works). (12 discs) Telefunken 6.35249, 6.35088.

**Galling, Martin. *9 Sonatas.* Vox SVBX-576 (3 discs). Sonatas 30, 42-47, 59, 60.

Gould, Glen. *6 Sonatas.* CBS 12M-36947(D). (2 dics) Sonatas 56, 58-62.

Kalish, Gilbert. *18 Sonatas.* Nonesuch 71318: Sonatas 31, 47, 53, 61. Nonesuch 71328: Sonatas 30, 32, 50. Nonesuch 71344: Sonatas 43, 49, 55, 59. Nonesuch 71362: Sonatas 33, 38, 54. Nonesuch 71379: Sonatas 29, 42, 45, 60.

**Klien, Walter. *11 Sonatas*. Vox SVBX 565 (3 discs). Sonatas 29, 31-3, 48-53, 62.

*McCabe, John. *Complete Sonatas*. London STS-15343/5; 15349/51; 15352/4; 15368/70; 15428/31. (16 discs).

**Neumeyer, Fritz. *17 Sonatas*. Vox SVBX-573 (clavichord and fortepiano) (3 discs). Sonatas 1-3, 5, 6, 8-18, 20.

**Kyniakou, Rena. *12 Sonatas*. Vox SVBX-574 (3 discs). Sonatas 35-41, 54-6, 58, 61.

*Shapiro, Joel. *6 Sonatas*. Orion 7141 (harpsichord). Sonatas 36-41.

*Shapiro, Joel. *1 Sonata*. Mark L-2(H-t). Sonata 59.

Svirsky, Sophie. *11 Sonatas*. Monitor S-2094/6 (3 discs). Sonatas 10, 32-4, 38, 42, 45, 47, 49, 53, 59.

Various Artists. *Complete Sonatas*, in: *Haydn, The Complete Solo Keyboard Music*. Hungaroton SLPX 11616-27 (12 discs).

----

*Currently out of print

**Note that the Vox recordings combine for a total of 50 of the 54 completed Sonatas that have survived. There are four releases with four different artists: Vol. I, Neumeyer; Vol. II, Kyniakou; Vol. III, Klien; and Vol. IV, Galling. These include the two "Raigern" Sonatas (Nos. 17 and 18, in the Neumeyer recording), plus all of the Sonatas in the older Peters Edition except No. 57 (H. 47).

Index of Musical Examples

Sonata (UE No.)	Example Number	Page
1	4	10
	48	72
4	5	11
	49	74
5	50	75
6	51	76
8	47	71
11	1	5
	2	5
	6	14
	7	15
	52	79
	53	80
	54	81
13	56	85
	57	86
	58	86
	59	87
15	60	88
30	8	18-20
	64	92
	65	92
31	9	21
	10	22
33	3	7
	11	24
	12	25
38	13	27
	14	28
	66	94-95
39	15	29

Sonata (UE No.)	Example Number	Page
41	16	30
42	17	31-32
46	18	34
	19	35
	20	35
47	21	36
	22	37
	23	38-39
49	24	40
53	25	42
	26	43
	27	44
	28	45
	29	46
	30	47
	61	89
	62	90
54	31	49
	63	90
55	31	49
57	55	90
59	33	49
	35	56-57
	37	59
	40	61
60	32	53
	36	58
	38	60
	41	62
62	34	55
	39	61
	42	63
	43	63
	44	64
	45	65
	46	66

Appendix

COLLATION OF HAYDN SONATA NUMBERS IN VARIOUS EDITIONS

Code

UE = Universal Edition (Vienna Urtext), 3 vols., 62 Sonatas (Numbering used in this book).
P = C. F. Peters edition, 4 vols., plus "Six Easy Divertimenti" (the latter indicated by the letter "D" preceding the Sonata number), 49 Sonatas total.
GS = G. Schirmer edition, 2 vols, 20 Sonatas.
K = Kalmus edition, 2 vols., 34 Sonatas (does not refer to the Kalmus reprint of the C. F. Peters edition, containing 43 Sonatas in 4 vols.)
He = G. Henle edition, 3 vols., 61 Sonatas.
H = Anthony von Hoboken Catalogue numbers, referring to Section XVI of the Catalogue unless otherwise noted.
Arabic numerals = consecutive Sonata numbers within an edition, except in the Henle edition, where they indicate page numbers. (Consecutive numbers are not assigned in the Henle edition.)
Roman numerals = volume number of an edition.

* = Thematic incipits only
** = Fragment
*** = Henle contains only the earlier version of this Sonata with a different slow movement (UE 19), which was previously unpublished

Number, Volume	UE Date	Key	P	GS	K	He	H
1 (I)	Before 1766	G	D-4			I-77	8
2	" "	C	D-5			I-74	7
3	" "	F	D-6			I-80	9
4	" "	G				I-90	(G) 1
5	" "	G	11 (I)			I-181	11
6	" "	C	43 (IV)			I-84	10
7	" "	D				I-94	XVII-D1
8	" "	A	23 (II)			I-6	5
9	" "	D	D-3			I-104	4
10	" "	C	D-1			I-68	1
11	" "	B♭	22 (II)			I-44	2
12	" "	A	29 (II)		26 (II)	I-14	12
13	" "	G	37 (IV)		31 (II)	I-34	6
14	" "	C	D-2			I-98	3
15	" "	E	18 (II)	17 (II)	17 (I)	I-19	13
16	" "	D	15 (II)	14 (II)	14 (I)	I-26	14
17	" "	E♭				I-53	
18	" "	E♭				I-60	
19	" "	e				I-180	
20	1766/67	B♭	19 (II)	18 (I)	18 (I)	I-162	18
21-27*	1767/68					I-180	
28**	165/66	D			23 (II)	I-143	XIV-5
29	1766	E♭	26 (III)			I-116	45
30	1767	D	9 (I)	9 (I)	9 (I)	I-130	19
31	1767/68	A♭	8 (I)	8 (I)	8 (I)	I-147	46

Number, Volume	UE Date	Key	P	GS	K	He	H
32	1768/70	g	4 (I)	4 (I)	4 (I)	I-171	44
33	1771	c	25 (III)		22 (II)	II-174	20
34	1771/73	D	20 (II)	19 (II)	19 (II)	III-12	33
35	1771/73	A♭	41 (IV)			III-1	43
36 (II)	1773	C	16 (II)	15 (II)	15 (I)	II-1	21
37	"	E	40 (IV)		34 (II)	II-12	22
38	"	F	21 (II)	20 (II)	20 (I)	II-22	23
39	"	D	31 (III)			II-34	24
40	"	E♭	32 (III)			II-44	25
41	"	A	33 (III)			II-52	26
42	1776	G	12 (II)	11 (II)	11 (I)	II-60	27
43	"	E♭	13 (II)	12 (II)	12 (I)	II-70	28
44	1774	F	14 (II)	13 (II)	13 (I)	II-82	29
45	1776	A	36 (IV)		30 (II)	II-96	30
46	"	E	30 (III)		27 (II)	II-106	31
47	"	b	39 (IV)		33 (II)	II-116	32
48	1777/79	C	5 (I)	5 (I)	5 (I)	II-126	35
49	"	c♯	6 (I)	6 (I)	6 (I)	II-138	36
50	"	D	7 (I)	7 (I)	7 (I)	II-146	37
51	"	E♭	35 (IV)		28 (II)	II-154	38
52	1780	G	17 (II)	16 (II)	16 (I)	II-162	39
53 (III)	1781/1782	e	2 (I)	2 (I)	2 (I)	III-22	34
54	1782/1784	G	26 (III)	10 (I)	10 (I)	III-33	40
55	"	B♭	27 (III)		24 (II)	III-40	41
56	"	D	28 (III)		25 (II)	III-48	42
57	1778	F	34 (IV)		28 (II)	•••	47
58	1788/89	C	24 (III)		21 (II)	III-56	48
59	1789/90	E♭	3 (I)	3 (I)	3 (I)	III-68	49
60	1794/95	C	42 (IV)			III-100	50
61	"	D	38 (IV)		32 (II)	III-114	51
62	1794	E♭	1 (I)	1 (I)	1 (I)	III-84	52

Index

Alfred Publishing Co., 70
Alpenheim, Ilse van, ii
American Music Teacher, ix
Aulabaugh, Alan, xi

Bach, C. P. E., 16; 23
Bach, J. S., 12; 21
    Inventions, 82
    Prelude In Eb Minor, 97
Beethoven, Ludwig van, vii; ix; xi; 2; 16; 23; 34; 36; 51; 67; 77; 96; 98; 101; 103
    Sonatas Op. 10, No. 1 & Op. 110, 84
    Sonatinas, 70
    String Quartet Op. 18, No. 5, 42
Boosey and Hawkes (Publisher), 4; 69
Breitkopf und Härtel (Publisher), 3; 4; 103
Brown, A. Peter, x; 101
Buchbinder, Rudolph, x

Chopin, Frédéric, 28; 65
Clementi, Muzio, 16; 70
Confletti, Donald, ix
Czerny, Carl, 81

Debussy, Claude
    Clair de lune, 87
Dussek, Jan Ladislav, 70

Edito Musico (Budapest Publisher), 4; 69
Esterhazy, 1; 52
    Princess, 48
European American Music Distributors Corp., xii; 3

Feder, Georg, 4; 69; 101

Geirenger, Karl, 50; 104

Haydn, Franz Joseph
    German Dances, 41
    International Haydn Conference, x
    London residencies, 52
    Oratorios, 52
    Piano Trios, 52
    "*Raigern*" *Sonatas*, (Sonatas 17 & 18), 103

Sonatas (UE Numbers)
    No. 1, 9-10; 70; 71-3; 84
    No. 2, 70
    No. 3, 70; 78
    No. 4, 10-12; 13; 71; 73-4; 76
    No. 5, 70; 71; 74-75; 79
    No. 6, 76-7
    No. 8, 71
    No. 9, 70
    No. 11, 5; 13-15; 78-81; 103
    No. 12, 103
    No. 13, 15; 84-7; 103
    No. 15, 87-8
    No. 17, 103
    No. 18, 103
    No. 19, 82; 113
    No. 30, 6; 16-20; 26; 33; 51; 87-8; 91-2; 98
    No. 31, 20-2; 26; 27; 33; 92-3; 98
    No. 32, 16; 98-9
    No. 33, 6; 16; 22-6; 35; 93; 96; 99
    No. 38, 26-8; 45; 93-5
    No. 39, 28-9
    No. 40, 31
    No. 41, 29-30
    No. 42, 31-3; 50; 81-2; 84; 88
    No. 44, 31
    No. 45, 31; 34
    No. 46, 33-5; 41-2; 46; 95-6
    No. 47, 35-9; 96
    No. 48, 41; 90-1
    No. 49, 16; 39-41; 48
    No. 50, 41; 87; 88-9; 91; 96-7
    No. 52, 41; 103
    No. 53, 42-8; 50; 87; 89; 97-8
    No. 54, 47; 48; 87; 89-90
    No. 55, 42; 48-50; 81; 82
    No. 56, 42; 48
    No. 57, 81-84
    No. 58, 16; 50-2; 67
    No. 59, 15; 52; 53-4; 55-60; 61; 67; 98
    No. 60, 52-3; 55-60; 61-2; 67
    No. 61, 52; 67
    No. 62, x; 52; 54-5; 60-1; 62-7; 99
String Quartets, ix; 1; 9; 13; 52; 101
    Opus 76, 67
Symphonies, 1; 9; 13; 101
    No. 104, 67
    London Symphonies, 52

Henle, G. (Publishers), 3-4; 69
Hernadi, Lajos, 4
Hoboken, Anthony van, 4; 103; 104
Hunt, John, vii

Jonas, Oswald, 3

Kraus, J. M., 103
Kuhlau, Frederich, 70

Landon, Christa, xii; 3; 101; 103; 104
Landon, H. C. Robbins, 50
    Collected Correspondence of Haydn, 103
Larsen, Jens Peter, 101

Martienssen, C. A., 3; 69
Monn, Matthias Georg, 9; 12
Mozart, Wolfgang A., vii; ix; xi; 16; 33; 70; 77; 98; 101
    Sonata in F, K. 279, 84
Music Teachers National Association, x

Newman, William S., x; 101
Nicholaus, Prince, 1

Palmer, Willard, 70
Päsler, Karl, 3; 4
Peters, C. F. (Publisher), ix; 3; 22; 69; 103

Rachmaninoff, Serge
    Prelude in C# Minor, 96-7
Reutter, Georg, 12

Schnaebel, Arthur, vii
Schotts, B. (Publishers), 4
Schubert, Franz, 16; 69; 70; 81
Simms, John, vii
Sturm und Dräng, 12; 15; 21-2; 26; 39; 41; 62; 91; 92; 93; 95; 96; 98

Tovey, Donald Francis, vii

Universal (Vienna Urtext) Edition, v; 3; 4; 22; 69; 86-7; 103; 104

Wagenseil, Georg Christoph, 9; 12

Studies in The History and Interpretation of Music

1. Hugo Meynell, **The Art of Handel's Operas**
2. Dale A. Jorgenson, **Moritz Hauptmann of Leipzig**
3. Nancy van Deusen, **The Harp and the Soul: Studies in Mediaeval Music**
4. James L. Taggart, **Franz Joseph Haydn's Keyboard Sonatas: An Untapped Gold Mine**
5. William E. Grim, **The Faust Legend in Music and Literature**
6. Richard R. La Croix (ed.), **Augustine on Music: An Interdisciplinary Collection of Essays**

ML 410 .H4 T25 1988

57756

Taggart, James L.
Franz Joseph Haydn's keyboard sonatas.